Ancient Monuments

SOUTHERN ENGLAND

MINISTRY OF PUBLIC BUILDING AND WORKS

ANCIENT MONUMENTS

in the care of the Ministry of Public Building and Works

Illustrated Regional Guide No. 2

SOUTHERN ENGLAND

by

The late LORD HARLECH

K.G., P.C., G.C.M.G., F.S.A.

Sometime First Commissioner of Works

LONDON
HER MAJESTY'S STATIONERY OFFICE
1970

First published 1936
Fourth edition 1970

SBN 11 670308 3

CONTENTS

ILLUSTRATIONS

PREFACE TO FIRST EDITION

In the preface to the first volume of this series of regional guides for visitors to the Ancient Monuments under the guardianship of the Office of Works I explained the scope and object of the series. The first edition of the first volume covering the six Northern Counties of England was sold out in a few weeks, and a second edition has now been issued.

Thus encouraged, I have written this second volume of the series, covering the monuments for which the Office is responsible in the counties south of the River Thames. I hope to include the remaining English monuments in the Midlands and East Anglia in a third volume, to be prepared in the course of this year, leaving Scotland and Wales to be dealt with separately at a later date.

In addition to the list of the monuments, county by county, giving the hours of opening and cost of admission to the public, and a map showing their whereabouts, and photographs of some of the most important, I have again provided in the form of an introduction a general description of the monuments in their chronological and historical settings. This survey is designed to help the ordinary visitor to understand what he or she is looking at.

The ever-increasing number of visitors to our national monuments shows that there is a growing circle of those who take a pride and interest in such things. For the sake of these visitors not only does the Department devote increasing care to the amenity and settings of the monuments but has prepared these regional guides and more technical handbooks to each of the more important individual monuments.

This second volume covers an area that contains such outstanding prehistoric monuments as Avebury, Stonehenge, and Maiden Castle. It includes the important Roman fortresses of

Richborough and Portchester, and the medieval castles of Dover and Carisbrooke. Whereas Volume I dealt with a number of abbeys and priories, only Netley in this volume is of the same order of importance as those in our Northern Counties. This volume, however, includes a number of interesting monuments that are at present less well known than they deserve, such as the very beautiful castle of Restormel in Cornwall, the romantic Tintagel, a number of Henry VIII's coast defence castles, and the delightful Queen's House at Greenwich built by Inigo Jones.

I should like to take this opportunity of acknowledging the assistance given me by independent archæologists as well as by the staff of my own Ancient Monuments Department in the preparation of these regional guides.

W. ORMSBY-GORE

OFFICE OF WORKS
April 1936

PREFACE TO SECOND EDITION

THIS series of guides to the Ancient Monuments of Great Britain under the care of the Ministry of Works was designed by Lord Harlech, and began to be published under his inspiration when he was the Rt. Hon. W. Ormsby-Gore, M.P., and First Commissioner of Works. He himself wrote the first three volumes, on Northern, Southern and Central England, which were issued in 1935–8. The fifth volume on North Wales, also written by him, was published in 1948. During the war the earlier volumes went out of print: this new edition has been brought up to date with the author's consent by the inclusion of additional monuments taken over since 1939, and by some revision in cases where the discovery of new evidence has led to a modification of previous theories. With these exceptions, however, the text in each case remains substantially that of the original author.

DAVID ECCLES
Minister of Works

MINISTRY OF WORKS
November 1951

PREFACE TO THIRD EDITION

ALL parts of the text have been thoroughly revised and brought up to date without violating the spirit and phraseology of the late Lord Harlech's work.

MINISTRY OF PUBLIC BUILDING AND WORKS
January 1966

PREFACE TO FOURTH EDITION

THOUGH the broadening of knowledge, as well as the number and scope of monuments in our guardianship have inevitably brought about a very extensive replacement of Lord Harlech's original text, it is a tribute to the culture and foresight of one who, in his political capacity as forerunner of the Minister of Public Building and Works, did so much to build up the Ancient Monuments Department that the shape and tenor of his work should still stand.

MINISTRY OF PUBLIC BUILDING AND WORKS
April 1970

PREHISTORIC PERIOD

From its geographical position in relation to the continent of Europe, the south of England naturally furnishes us with the evidence of successive influences which, either by trade or by invasion, affected the population of England from the earliest times to the Roman conquest.

As this is a guide to monuments, and not an archæological treatise, it is unnecessary to trace layer by layer the full story from the earliest evidences of human occupation in our island, and it must suffice to begin with the period of our earliest monuments, which date from the Neolithic or Late Stone Age probably beginning a little before 4000 B.C.

Neolithic

The arrival from more than one source of new peoples with a neolithic culture effected a profound revolution in Britain. They were the first comers to our island to own domestic animals, to cultivate the soil with grain crops, to make pottery, to grind and polish stone implements as well as to chip them, to construct defensible enclosures, and finally, though not perhaps at the beginning of their occupation, to erect monuments to their important dead in the style known as "megalithic", involving the use of huge blocks of stone. Almost any one of these advances would have marked a revolution in human progress, but the evidence suggests that all, except the last, reached Britain somewhere about the same time, by the convergence of several streams of migration from continental Europe. These peoples found on the chalk downs, the limestone wolds and the gravel plains, but not on the densely-wooded clays, conditions very suitable for settlement and for the life which their knowledge then enabled them to lead. It is thus mainly along the uplands of the south and south-east that we find evidence of neolithic culture in the form of flint-mines, long barrows, and enclosures, usually on hill-tops, of the type known as "causewayed camps" which are peculiar to this period. One such causewayed camp has been identified beneath the later Iron Age fortifications of *Maiden Castle* in Dorset (Plate 4) and another at *Windmill Hill* near *Avebury*.

The archæological evidence would seem to point to two main sources of intrusion. First, from Portugal and Spain, probably by way of Brittany, to our south-west coasts, as also to Wales, Ireland, western and extreme northern Scotland. Second, from Switzerland and eastern France, where we find the continental parallels to our causewayed camps, and smooth pottery like that called "Windmill Hill" ware, which takes its name from the first large habitation-site of this period to be carefully examined and where it was found in quantity.

The simplest, but not necessarily the earliest, of the megalithic tomb-structures are the so-called "Dolmens"—chambers consisting of a gigantic horizontal capstone resting on a polygonal group of large upright stones. Many, perhaps all, of those standing free today were originally inside burial mounds or "barrows", from which the earth has been eroded over at least four thousand years. Their predominantly Atlantic distribution— Portugal, Brittany, Cornwall, Ireland, Anglesey—associates them with the first of the above-mentioned courses of intrusion.

Trethevy Quoit in Cornwall (Plate 2) is a typical monument of this class in our guardianship. There is also a distinct group of monuments of the same general class in Kent, of which *Kit's Coty House* and the ruinous *Little Kit's Coty House*, nearby, are in our guardianship. Of these the former was originally embedded in a long barrow, *i.e.* one of oval or wedge-shaped plan, and the other in a more compact mound.

There is a much larger group of long barrows containing more complicated megalithic burial chambers in a broad continuous belt from the southern Cotswolds to the Dorset coast; three of them, all of the same general plan, which are in the Ministry's guardianship, lie south of the Thames and Avon. These are *Wayland's Smithy* in Berkshire, *West Kennet* near *Avebury* in Wiltshire, and *Stoney Littleton* near Wellow in Somerset. *Wayland's Smithy*, near Ashbury, is much denuded and its chambers are partly exposed. It was excavated in 1919–20 and again in 1962, when a smaller and simpler long barrow was detected within it. *West Kennet*—one of the biggest in Britain—was excavated in 1859 according to the limited methods of the time and more thoroughly and with modern technique in 1955–6; *Stoney Littleton* has its chambers largely intact and completely covered by the mound. It is also a monument to the "prehistory of prehistory", having been excavated in 1816 and restored in 1858, with a skill astonishing for this date, and handed into our guardianship in 1884, immediately after the first Ancient Monuments Act.

It is generally thought that the long barrows with terminal chambers, including the three afore-mentioned, are the earliest, those with side chambers and a "false door" are later, and the "passage graves" (see Bronze Age section) are later still. But one of the most frequent causes of archæological uncertainty is the common re-use of barrows for secondary burials in later ages. The same barrows were often used as sacred repositories for the remains of the dead by successive peoples from Neolithic to Saxon times, and it is sometimes difficult to be sure from the finds in them that the original or primary use has been identified.

The next large-scale intrusion, from the Rhineland and Brittany early in the second millennium B.C., was that of the people known as the "Beaker Folk", from their characteristic decorated pottery. They buried their dead in a crouched position often under round barrows. During the period in which they were dominant the earliest bronze tools and weapons were introduced by trade, and the Beaker folk are sometimes included in the Early Bronze Age in Britain.

Bronze Age

THE Beaker people first landed on the southern and eastern coasts of Britain and gradually spread to and occupied other parts of the country. Finds of actual beakers would seem to show that

the occupation was more intensive in certain clearly defined areas:
(1) The Yorkshire Wolds (2) The Peak district of Derbyshire
(3) The eastern edges of the Fens and parts of the East Anglian
coast (4) Wessex (5) The Thames estuary and valley and (6)
Northumberland and eastern Scotland.

In Wessex, at the end of the Beaker period, the appearance of
a rich warrior group from Brittany opened up extensive trade
relations, which brought amber from the Baltic, gold and bronze
from Ireland, and blue faïence beads perhaps from as far away as
Egypt. The members of the new aristocracy were buried in a
distinctive form of round barrow, the bell barrow, which has a
conical mound and a carefully made ditch encircling it, leaving
a flat area or berm between the two. A variety, the disc barrow,
perhaps reserved for women, has a very small central mound
and a correspondingly wide berm. The ditch, like a "Henge"
monument (see below), usually has a bank outside it. A group of
typical Wessex barrows, including bell and disc types, is in our
guardianship at *Winterborne Poor Lot*, Dorset.

It is, however, to the Beaker folk, after they had made contact
with the Neolithic builders of megalithic tombs, that we can
probably ascribe the initiation of our most spectacular prehistoric remains, the great stone circles. Everything seems to
point to their responsibility for the great "temple" at *Avebury*,
with its avenues, and for elements at *Stonehenge*—and, if these,
then probably also *Stanton Drew* and perhaps other examples.
A characteristic of these three monuments is that the stones are
encircled by a ditch and bank, and this is the feature which has
given the archæological term "Henge", on the analogy of
Stonehenge, to a large class of such monuments, though, curiously,
Stonehenge is the only one to have its bank inside the ditch.
Where no suitable stone was available the circle of uprights
within the ditch could be of timber, as excavation has shown it to
have been at *Woodhenge* and Arminghall near Norwich. At
Knowlton only the bank and ditch remain and the uprights may
likewise have been of wood. "Henge" earthworks go back to
the Neolithic period, but finds of Beaker pottery as at *Avebury*
and *Woodhenge* and the general distribution of "Henge" monuments would indicate that the majority of them were still in use

during the Beaker period. They are in fact found in all the areas of Beaker concentration enumerated above, and some of them contain stone circles in all the areas except Yorkshire, East Anglia and the Lower Thames, where timber circles would seem to have sufficed. On the other hand, megalithic circles, sometimes with "Henge" earthworks, also occur in parts where Beaker penetration is either not attested, or very sparse, such as Cornwall south-west Wales and even the Orkneys.

The conclusion which one is inclined to draw from the available data is that the megalithic "idea" was introduced to our shores by maritime adventurers from the Mediterranean *via* Portugal and Brittany, but that it required the political capacity and organizing power of the Beaker folk to translate this "idea" into such major works as *Avebury, Stonehenge*, and *Stanton Drew* early in the second millenium B.C. It also seems likely that the practice lingered in less ambitious form long after the Beaker occupation, and the veneration which such mighty remains must have inspired in subsequent generations may have led to imitation throughout the Bronze Age.

The greatest of all stone circles is *Avebury* (Plate 1), placed under the guardianship of the Ministry of Public Building and Works by the National Trust. Its circle of very large blocks of sarsen contained two other smaller circles, and was surrounded by a fosse or ditch 50 feet deep and a huge bank outside it. Much of the modern village is within the great circle, and the breaking up of the megaliths for building purposes in the eighteenth and nineteenth centuries has done much to diminish the spectacular appearance of the monument. But it is the largest prehistoric circle in the world, and enough is still visible to justify the dictum of Stukeley, the eighteenth-century antiquary, that "Avebury is to Stonehenge as a cathedral is to a parish church".

From the main circle an avenue of stones led south-eastwards towards the village of West Kennet. The northern end of this avenue has been excavated and any stones found have been re-erected in their former positions, and the sites of the missing stones have been determined and marked, with the result that enough can now be seen to give a very fair impression of its original appearance. The avenue terminated on Overton Hill in a small circle known as the *Sanctuary*, which is in our guardian-ship. This consisted of two concentric circles of stones and six of timber uprights. The circles have now disappeared, but the sites of the stones and of the timbers are marked. It has been suggested that the *Sanctuary* was a roofed structure built in four phases. Originally, it seems, there was only a small round hut, possibly sacred in nature, with a conical roof. In the next phase a circular roofed building, open at the centre, seems to have been built to enclose the hut. In the third phase the earlier structures were cleared away, and replaced by what may have been a large roofed temple, with standing stones between the posts of an inner colonnade, and an entrance towards *Avebury*. In the final phase a large outer circle of stones was erected, and these were joined to the end of the West Kennet Avenue.

About a mile and a half west of the *Sanctuary* beside the main Bath road stands *Silbury Hill*, also in our guardianship. It is the largest circular artificial mound in Europe, and may possibly be connected in date and in purpose with *Avebury*, though the results of such excavations as have been made at various times are inconclusive. About half a mile to the south is the great *West Kennet* long barrow already mentioned.

Windmill Hill lies about a mile and a half to the north-west of *Avebury*. It is a prehistoric occupation-site of the greatest importance, covering a large causewayed camp of Neolithic type. It was partially excavated in the 1920s, the first extensive and scientific examination of such a site. As such it provided a chronological series of artefacts from the middle Neolithic to the Beaker period that has formed the basis of subsequent studies of this period. Many are exhibited at *Avebury Museum*.

The whole Avebury group affords the most remarkable evidence of the organization attained by the Beaker folk. These mighty works must, with the means at their command, have involved a marshalling of labour and an intensity of purpose of a most exceptional kind. *Silbury Hill* alone must have involved the work of hundreds of men for a long time, seeing that the hard chalk had to be loosened with picks made of stone or of the antlers of the red deer, and either carried in baskets or shovelled up with implements formed from the shoulder-blade bones

Plate 1. Avebury

Plate 2. Trethevy Quoit

Plate 3. Stonehenge

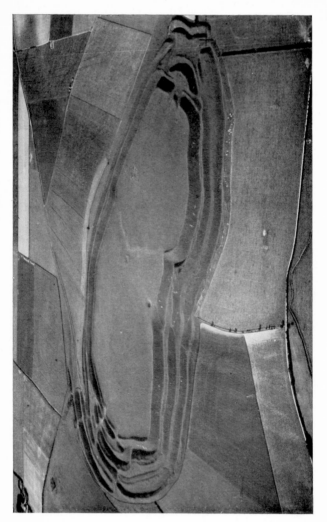

Plate 4. Maiden Castle

of animals. The digging of the great fosse at *Avebury* itself must have been a task far bigger than the dragging of the large sarsen monoliths in hundreds from the neighbouring downs, and erecting them with no little mathematical precision. That the purpose was religious there can be little doubt.

If *Avebury* is the greatest, *Stonehenge* (Plate 3) is undoubtedly the most famous of British stone circles.* It is now the property of the Ministry of Public Building and Works. Its sophistication when compared with all other stone circles, the presence of the " blue " stones, brought almost certainly by sea all the way from Prescelly in Pembrokeshire (another centre of megalithic activity), the unique trilithons with their mortice and tenon joints, and many other features make *Stonehenge* a monument, though small in scale compared with the *Avebury* complex, that excites the wonder and speculation of scientist and amateur alike. Just as *Avebury* is but the centre of a great variety of other important prehistoric remains, so *Stonehenge* is surrounded with the traces of avenues and innumerable barrows long and round. *Avebury* and *Stonehenge* alone make Wiltshire the most significant area in prehistoric England; and here too we have the remains or records of no fewer than eighty long and 2,000 round barrows, as well as early prehistoric camps, flint mines, etc., in numbers and interest such as no other area can rival.

Some two miles north-east of *Stonehenge* is another circle in our guardianship known as *Woodhenge*, near Durrington. Its discovery, in 1925, was one of the first triumphs of the archæological use of air-photography and on excavation it was found to be a typical " Henge " monument with six concentric circles of timber uprights, of which the positions are marked as at the *Sanctuary*. In the area of the central ring was found the crouched skeleton of a child whose skull had been cleft through—probably a dedicatory sacrifice. *Woodhenge*, like the *Sanctuary*, was perhaps also a roofed structure, but in the form of a circular gallery

---

*It should not be necessary to emphasize that neither *Stonehenge* nor any other stone circle had originally the smallest connection with the Druids, whose cult was not introduced into Britain till most of the stone circles were a thousand years old.

with ridged roof, the whole open in the centre. The central area would serve for the performance of ceremonies and rites.

Another complex of megalithic stone circles and avenues is at *Stanton Drew* in Somerset. This and the adjacent structure known as the *Cove* are in our guardianship. There are three circles, the largest of which probably originally consisted of thirty stones, twenty-seven of which remain, but only three are still standing; the smallest was of eight stones, seven still upright; and the third was originally of twelve stones, all fallen. The two former circles are approached by converging avenues. No scientific excavation has yet been undertaken at *Stanton Drew*, which of all stone circles bears the most striking analogies with *Avebury*. Two more stone circles in our guardianship are that at *Kingston Russell* and the small one known as the *Nine Stones* at Winterborne Abbas. Both are in Dorset between Dorchester and Bridport.

The development of Cornwall followed rather different lines from those of Wessex. No causewayed camps have yet been identified in the Duchy, and though the typical neolithic long barrow is found, and dolmens such as *Trethevy Quoit*, the characteristic early sepulchres of Cornwall dating from the Late Neolithic or earliest Bronze Age are the chambered barrows and passage graves of types found mainly in Portugal, Brittany, Wales, and Ireland. The Scilly Isles have no fewer than forty-three chambered barrows as against fifteen in Cornwall, mostly at its extreme western end, pointing to the use of the islands as an important maritime entrepôt during the second millenium B.C. Four of the best of the tombs of Scilly—*Bants Carn*, *Porth Hellick Down*, *Innisidgen* and *Lower Innisidgen*—are in the guardianship of the Ministry, as is a round chambered tomb of unusual type at *Ballowall* on the western tip of the mainland.

The cultural and trading connections of Cornwall were likewise with countries accessible by sea, especially Brittany and Ireland. Gold lunulae, or crescent-shaped collars, made in Ireland in the Early Bronze period, occur in Cornwall, and pottery of the same period tells a like story. The types found in the rest of Britain are unknown, but the typical Cornish vessels, bi-conical, with cord-impressions and usually two lugs, are also found in Brittany and Ireland, but hardly ever in England proper.

Despite these differences Cornwall has a considerable number of megalithic circles. There are at least sixteen known in the Duchy, seven concentrated in the extreme west, and nine in a fairly compact group in the region of Bodmin Moor. Among these "*The Hurlers*", three large circles in a line, near St. Cleer, are in our guardianship; and a round barrow close to them produced a rich early Bronze Age burial.

After the great outpouring of energy in the Late Neolithic and Early Bronze ages, which culturally and economically belong together, despite the introduction of new materials and the influx of new peoples, the inhabitants of England seem to have settled down to centuries of relative isolation undisturbed by large-scale movements. But fairly late in the Bronze Age we are presented with widespread evidence of an intrusive culture in Southern England, practising more intensive cultivation. It derived from Central Europe, and is usually called the Urnfield Culture, from its characteristic cemeteries of cremation burials in urns set in flat graves. In England it spread slowly, and its influence was felt mostly in Wessex. In this country it is often referred to as the "Deverel-Rimbury" culture, from the names of two Wessex burial-sites.

It was probably in the epoch of the late Bronze Age that Cornish tin began to be worked on a scale that might have been sufficient for trade overseas, and such workings are associated with remains closely akin to those of the "Deverel-Rimbury" culture. Although there is evidence of tin having been worked before this time, much of the bronze used in England in the latter part of the Bronze Age must have been made with Cornish tin.

Our knowledge of the Bronze Age is mainly drawn from the round barrow burials which are so frequent on the open uplands of southern England. Few permanent habitation sites of this period have been found. The causewayed camps of an earlier period were no longer occupied, and the evidence from the uplands generally suggests pastoral or semi-nomadic habits; cattle-enclosures are found in Cranborne Chase and on the Marlborough Downs. On Dartmoor, however, many villages of this period have been found, consisting of groups of stone-built huts with small cultivated plots, which prove an occupation of this region denser than at any later age. These conditions were doubtless favoured by the warm dry climate of the Bronze Age, at the end of which there was a sudden change to damper conditions which induced the very different habits of the succeeding age.

Iron Age

WHEN exactly the first iron-using peoples came to Britain is difficult to determine; probably rather after 750 B.C. Sometime after this date until the expansion of the Roman Empire the dominating fact of Central Europe was the power and mobility of the Celtic tribes. Archæologists have divided this long period of Iron Age development into two main phases called "Hallstatt" and "La Tène". The former takes its name from a great necropolis in Austria, the latter from a celebrated archæological site on the lake of Neuchâtel in Switzerland. La Tène rises to prominence as Hallstatt declines. In both we find the evolution of new types of pottery, of new weapons and implements of both bronze and iron, and ultimately of Celtic art and decoration which seems to owe motives, stylized in a characteristically Celtic way, to Ancient Greece and the Scythians.

In this country the Pre-Roman Iron Age can best be treated under "Earlier" and "Later" phases. In the non-Romanized parts Iron-age culture lingered much longer.

EARLIER PRE-ROMAN IRON AGE

IN the seventh century B.C. there began on the continent of Europe a great expansion of Iron Age tribes perhaps caused by pressure from Germanic peoples moving south from the region of the Baltic. In the district of the lower Rhine, a mixed Celto–Germanic people resulted, who in later times were known as the Belgæ, and had an enormous influence on the history of Britain.

In the late sixth century B.C. a further expansion of the Iron Age tribes, who were just then beginning to develop the La Tène culture, disturbed those peoples of Gaul and the Low Countries who were still in the Hallstatt phase and some may have migrated into Italy, Spain and Britain. Thus somewhere about 500–450 B.C. there began the immigration into Britain of small groups of people, of both sexes, in the late Hallstatt stage of culture, and possibly Celtic-speaking, who established the Iron Age civilization all over lowland England from Weymouth to the Wash, and on the coast of Yorkshire. The majority of these people probably came from the Rhineland and the Netherlands, but others came from the valley of the Marne.

Under these invaders, or just before, in the final phase of the Bronze Age, there was a return to permanent habitation on the uplands, and instead of a pastoral nomadic people, a settled, agricultural population is attested by the "Celtic" field systems that have been discovered over a wide area, largely by air-photography. On the uplands, sometimes overlying the sites of causewayed camps, these peoples built great hill-forts defended by formidable ramparts of earth, sometimes laced with timber or faced with rough stonework. The number and size of these hill-top fortress camps in Wiltshire and Dorset is remarkable. That they were the strongholds of tribal groups seems probable, and this seems to point to a phase of tribal consolidation and consequent warlike activity and defensive needs of which there are few signs in the preceding Bronze Age. The construction, and often the enlargement, of these camps continued through the centuries right up to the Roman invasion.

In the southern region five of these early Iron Age camps are in the guardianship of the Ministry, namely, *Maiden Castle*, Dorset; *Bratton Camp*, Westbury, Wiltshire; *Blackbury Castle* near Southleigh in Devon; *Uffington Castle*, Berkshire; and also the outer works of *Old Sarum*, though they have been considerably altered. In addition it has been convincingly argued that the outer earthworks of *Dover Castle* (see Medieval Section) preserve the line of a large Iron Age hill-fort.

From about 300 B.C. new bands of migrants were arriving in Britain from northern Gaul. Their earliest settlements have been detected on the south coast as well as on the east; some of the more south-westerly seem once again to point to contacts with

Brittany and the Atlantic coast of Europe. They were probably not homogeneous, but they had reached a developed stage of La Tène culture. It was these people who were responsible for the introduction into this country of what is popularly recognized as Celtic art. Their bronzes and pottery were frequently decorated with scroll work and those stylized "palmette" patterns which survived even the long Roman occupation, and revived again in the Dark Ages before the Norman Conquest.

During this period hill-forts were constructed with more elaborate fortifications, and, where stone was available, the use of stone facings became more prevalent. Among the largest are Hembury in Devon and Ham Hill in Somerset. But the most stupendous of all such forts is *Maiden Castle* (Plate 4), where the existing gigantic earthworks were erected early in the last century B.C. The multiplication of lines of rampart and ditch seen at *Maiden Castle*, and other large hill-forts in Wessex, seems to have been against the attacks by means of slings with a range of up to a hundred yards. When used defensively the slingers were stationed on platforms near the gates, and their ammunition was stored in pits behind the defences—one such sling-stone dump at *Maiden Castle* contained over 22,000 selected beach pebbles. At *Blackbury Castle*, near Southleigh in Devon; the triangular outworks to the entrance were probably added in later Iron Age times to the single bank and ditch of the original camp.

Among the most interesting relics of these people in southern England are the waterside settlements at Glastonbury and Meare, where highly developed products of their art have been discovered. These are now mostly preserved in the Taunton Museum and in the museum in the *Tribunal* at *Glastonbury* (see Medieval Section). Open villages of this period are also fairly numerous in Cornwall, generally within the shelter of a hill-fort; one variety is confined to the extreme western peninsula of Penwith. Two such villages are in our guardianship, namely, *Chysauster*, about three miles north of Penzance, and *Carn Euny*, about four and a half miles west of Penzance, *Chysauster* seems to have originated in the first century A.D., and it continued in occupation under the Roman Empire up to the third century A.D.

The houses consist of oval enclosures of thick dry-built masonry, forming an open court from which various rooms open: the shape is common to other Cornish villages of this type. *Chysauster* and *Carn Euny*, like other such villages, contain a curious underground chamber known locally as "fogou" and possibly used for food-storage. Parallels to these are found in Scotland and Ireland.

It is to this period that the great age of the tin mines of Cornwall belongs. Merchants from the Greek city of Massilia (Marseilles) were certainly engaged in the tin trade in the fourth and third centuries, but their activities may concern the region about the mouth of the Loire, rather than Britain. The archæological evidence suggests that the great period for the exploitation of Cornish tin was during the last two or three centuries B.C. It is important to remember that the Romans did not mine the tin of Cornwall before A.D. 250 and then only very little, and that the Romanizing of the Duchy was only partial. Neither Strabo nor Pliny mentions tin as an export of Cornwall in the first century A.D., and Cæsar heard of it only at second-hand from the Kentish tribes, who told him it came from the "interior".

LATER PRE-ROMAN IRON AGE

IN the last century B.C. groups of Belgæ, whom we have already noticed in the region of the lower Rhine moved into Britain. They had spread over north-eastern France during the preceding centuries, and had absorbed the culture of La Tène, and early in the last century B.C. some of them crossed to Britain, where they occupied the south-eastern districts (with the exception of Sussex), influencing the earlier Iron Age peoples. They may have been set in motion by the great Cimbric disturbance of the end of the second century.

Between 58 and 56 B.C. when Julius Cæsar was engaged in conquering Gaul, the Belgæ of Britain on several occasions sent help to their kinsmen across the Channel. This led to Cæsar's two invasions of 55 and 54 B.C., the first being merely a reconnaissance, and the second a punitive expedition, when Cæsar penetrated beyond the Thames, and defeated Cassivellaunus, chief of the Belgic tribe of the Catuvellauni, to whose command the other chieftains had submitted in order to oppose the invader. After his victory Cæsar imposed tribute on the British tribes, but it does not appear that any serious attempt was made to collect it: his invasions, however, seem to have achieved their object, and we hear no more of British interference in Gaul. On the contrary, the Roman conquest of Gaul led to a fresh invasion of Britain by Belgic refugees from the Roman power. One, Commius, chief of the Atrebates (who give their name to Arras) had been a loyal ally of Cæsar in Gaul; but in 52 B.C. he joined the great Gallic rebellion against Rome, and on its failure he became an outlaw, and early in 50 B.C. he escaped to Britain with numerous followers from his own Atrebates and other Belgæ. He established himself in the country between Southampton Water and the Thames, and brought it under the rule of himself and his descendants, thus effecting a second Belgic invasion.

Although recognized by Cæsar as more barbarous and warlike than the other peoples of Gaul, the Belgæ already possessed many of the attributes of civilization when they reached southern Britain. Cultural progress in these parts during the century between Cæsar's invasion and that of Claudius was rapid. Though the Belgæ built hill-forts, these seem mostly to be purely military works concentrated on frontiers rather than the tribal capitals of the earlier stages of the Iron Age. Their urban centres were on plateau sites such as *Silchester*, the seat of the house of Commius on the Hampshire–Berkshire border, or the successive capitals of the Catuvellaunian princes at *Verulamium* (St. Albans) and Colchester and they were protected by far-flung lines of earthworks. A trend towards larger social groups than the tribe was now recognizable. Already in Cæsar's time Cassivellaunus was recognized as leader in war of all the tribes affected by the invasion: early in the first century A.D. his ultimate successor Cunobelin asserted his supremacy over almost the whole of south-eastern England and greatly reduced the dominions of his Belgic rival, the house of Commius. British princes abandoned the barbarous coinage which the earlier Belgæ had produced, and took to striking coins on the Roman model with Roman inscriptions, and called themselves by the Latin title *Rex*, and goods of Roman manufacture were quite common in the markets of Belgic Britain.

Cunobelin's long reign (about A.D. 5–40) was thus a period of cultural development, though his aggressions made him enemies among the other chieftains, Belgic and non-Belgic, and caused them to look for succour towards Rome.

Of monuments under our guardianship, little can be ascribed to the Belgæ except the final modifications of certain hill-forts, especially *Maiden Castle*. The *White Horse* of Uffington, probably the only really ancient member of the series of horses cut in the turf of the chalk downs, has also generally been thought to date from this time, because of its resemblance to the stylized horse on the reverse of Celtic imitations of gold staters of Philip of Macedon, at first imported from Gaul but struck also in Britain after the arrival of the Belgæ. But it has been observed that the *White Horse* has changed shape with soil erosion and grown more "Belgic-looking" with the years, so that its present appearance may be fortuitous and its traditional ascription to the Anglo-Saxons may be correct after all. *Bratton Camp* also has an adjacent White Horse. In its present form it dates from the eighteenth century, but it is possible that there was an earlier horse on or near the site.

We have written in the above survey of successive intrusions of peoples who introduced new cultures and ways of life into southern and eastern Britain, cultures which were only slowly absorbed in the north and west. In view of the probability that few of these invasions were in the nature of mass migrations, and also of the probability that few women accompanied their menfolk in the hazard of the seas, it is almost certain that by the close of the prehistoric period the population of Britain was already of very mixed race, though all or most may have adopted Celtic speech. Cæsar himself noted the contrast between the tall fair-haired elements and the short dark-haired. Clearly many strains from Neolithic and Early Bronze Age times survived in the ranks below the aristocracy of Celtic warrior chiefs.

Throughout prehistoric times the greater part of the lowlands and valleys of England were densely forested, and until iron came into general use man could make little headway against the forest. Until the latter part of the pre-Roman Iron Age the potter's wheel and wheeled vehicles were unknown. Horses and cattle were small in stature compared with those of today. But the earliest Neolithic occupants of the *Avebury* area already possessed them, as well as pigs, goats and hunting dogs.

Despite the wealth of data made available by improvements in archæological method over more than two generations, and not least in southern England which is particularly rich in prehistoric remains, it is still too soon to present a survey of British pre-history with any claims to finality. In order to complete the picture of which we can at present only offer an outline sketch, we must be careful to avoid considering the problems of the south British, or any other area in isolation, but endeavour to interpret the results of excavation in this area in the light of knowledge obtained from places as far apart as Portugal and Denmark, or the Outer Hebrides and the Rhine. Nothing is more remarkable than the wide diffusion of the evidences of similar cultures during prehistoric ages, and it is only by the scientific collation of these that we can tell at all accurately the story of the earliest colonization of Britain by our remote predecessors.

ROMAN PERIOD

THE two invasions of Julius Cæsar belong in effect to the preceding period of British history, and have been mentioned in
that context. For nearly a hundred years after them Britain was
left alone by the Roman Government, until the peaceful penetration of Roman traders and the hostile rivalries of British
chieftains made the time ripe for the annexations which Julius
had dreamed of and Augustus on two occasions contemplated.

In A.D. 43 the Emperor Claudius gave orders for the invasion
of Britain, and an army of four legions, with auxiliaries, was
landed under the command of Aulus Plautius Silvanus.

One of their ports of disembarkation was certainly *Richborough*
(Portus Rutupiæ) (Plate 5), which is in our guardianship. Here
among the successive traces of occupation lasting four centuries
can be seen part of the fortifications thrown up by the legions
of Aulus Plautius to protect their base on landing.

The objective of the conquest was the Catuvellaunian kingdom.
The other chieftains who had suffered from Cunobelin expansion
might welcome it, and would be allowed to remain as subject
allies of Rome. Among them was Cogidubnus, perhaps the heir
to the realms of Commius, who was established or confirmed
in his domains in west Sussex, where an inscription at Chichester
records his privileged status as "King and Legate of the
Emperor". He almost certainly built the palace at Fishbourne,
near Chichester, whose remains are in the care of the Sussex
Archæological Trust.

The resistance of the Catuvellauni, though fierce, was soon
crushed by the capture of their capital near Colchester (Camulo-
dunum). Once the main Belgic power had been broken, the
south and west subjugation followed fairly easily. It was entrusted
to the Second Legion, then under the command of the future
Emperor Vespasian, who, we are told by Suetonius, captured
twenty British hill-forts in the course of this campaign. These

must have included Hod Hill in Dorset, where an efficiently fortified Roman camp was built within the massive but clumsy ramparts, and *Maiden Castle*, which the Romans stormed and "slighted".

The Roman conquest though rapid was complete. Within five years of the first invasion the Romans were mining the lead of the Mendips, and there was no further military activity south of the Thames for at least 150 years.

The achievements of the Roman Empire during that period, were the victories of peace. Local government was instituted, according to the Roman practice in Gaul, on the basis of the existing tribal divisions, each tribe having its own territory with a capital town. In southern England there were six such tribal states—the Cantiaci of Kent, capital Canterbury (Durovernum), the Atrebates of Berkshire, Surrey, and north Hampshire, capital *Silchester* (Calleva), the Belgæ, a federation of Belgic groups extending from Hampshire to north Somerset, capital Winchester (Venta), the Regnenses of Sussex, capital Chichester (Noviomagus), the Durotriges of Dorset, capital Dorchester (Dornovaria), and the Dumnonii of the far west, capital Exeter (Isca). Five of these towns are covered by modern cities and the piece-meal recovery of their Roman plans has been the patient work of recent archæology. But the sixth, *Silchester*, is unencumbered, and was systematically excavated in the nineteenth century and recently, in part, re-examined. Plans and many of the finds are preserved in Reading Museum. The buildings included a small Christian church of the fourth century. This and the chapel at *Lullingstone*, where fragmentary figured wall-paintings were found, are among the few monuments of Christian cult in Roman Britain. The only structures at *Silchester* standing above ground, are the town walls, which date from the late second or early third century, and form a complete circuit apart from the gates. They have been placed in our guardianship by the Duke of Wellington.

Conspicuous among the monuments of the Roman age in Britain are the villas which are numerous in the southern counties and which continued to flourish in the fourth century, when other aspects of the Empire showed signs of dissolution. The palatial villa at Fishbourne is unique, but among the larger examples may be mentioned *Lullingstone*, Darenth and Folkestone in Kent (the first-named being in our guardianship) Bignor in Sussex, and Brading in the Isle of Wight. It is, of course, a mistake to suppose that these villas were inhabited by immigrant Romans from Italy. They were the farms and houses of well-to-do British-born gentry, whose ancestors had fought against Cæsar and Claudius; and it was the greatest achievement of the Empire to turn such people into Romans.

Perhaps the most important factor in the "Romanizing" of the country was the road system. The great majority of the main Roman roads were laid out by military engineers to meet the needs of the army during the period of conquest. This is exemplified in eastern Kent where four roads from the four ports of *Reculver*, *Richborough*, Dover, and Lympne converge on Canterbury, whence the road now known as Watling Street (most of which is still in use) proceeds direct to the crossing of the Thames at Southwark. But when once their military purpose had been served the roads remained as a civilizing agency of the first importance, and it is worth notice that the centre of the road-system was London. In south England, apart from those highways already mentioned, roads ran from London to Chichester and to *Silchester*, where four routes diverged to Gloucester, Bath, and Winchester, Old Sarum, and Dorchester. Few Roman roads are more striking to-day than the section of the Dorchester road beyond Old Sarum striding over Oakley Down in north Dorset, and cutting through Bronze Age barrows in its path. This section is scheduled as an ancient monument.

During this period of consolidation and relative peace, the original base-camp at *Richborough* had undergone several changes. Shortly after the first landing the site became a military depot and numbers of large store-houses and other buildings in timber were erected. Towards the end of the first century these buildings were swept away and a great monument was built, probably to commemorate the conquest of Britain. This consisted of four massive piers carrying arches, and a sculptured composition above them. The huge concrete foundation preserved the pattern of the paths running under the arches and intersecting. The monument was cased with slabs of imported Italian marble, and bore an inscription, too little of which has been found to make a restoration possible. During the second and third centuries civilian buildings grew up in the shadow of it.

In the latter part of the third century military activity again became necessary in the south owing to the raids of Saxon pirates, and as a result a small fort was established at *Richborough* around the monument; the triple ditches of this fort have been excavated and are now left open. Shortly afterwards a larger area was enclosed by the existing stone fort, the walls of which remain up to 25 feet high in places, and are no less than 11 feet thick. Its plan was rectangular, and the wall was strengthened by turrets, and surrounded by a double ditch. A comprehensive selection of the important finds made during the excavations of the 1920s is shown in the museum on the site.

This stone fort at *Richborough* (Rutupiae) was one of a series of similar forts erected at about this time to guard the east and south coasts from Saxon raids. In the fourth century most of them were under the command of a special officer with the title of "Count of the Saxon Shore". Three other forts of this Saxon Shore series in the southern counties besides *Richborough* are under our guardianship, namely *Reculver* (Regulbium), *Pevensey* (Anderida), and *Portchester* (probably Portus Adurni).

Reculver is typologically the earliest of the series; recent exploration has demonstrated that a fort existed there early in the third century; there was previous occupation of the site from the late Iron Age onwards. *Pevensey* (Plate 7) seems to be substantially later than the other three, and to date from the fourth century, when the Count of the Saxon Shore was already in office; it is oval, not rectangular, and its walls are provided with solid semicircular bastions. The masonry is similar to that of the other but of even finer quality. As late as 1147 when *Pevensey* was besieged by King Stephen, it proved impregnable because of the strength of "its most ancient walls". William the Conqueror had landed at *Pevensey*, and before the end of the eleventh century the Normans had begun the construction within the large Roman fortress of an inner bailey and keep, but clearly it was the old

Roman curtain then still intact which made the place impregnable in those days.

The existing appearance of *Portchester* (Plate 6) is even more impressive than *Pevensey*. In fact, next to Hadrian's Wall it is the most remarkable Roman monument in Britain. High tides in Portsmouth Harbour still reach the foot of the great Roman walls with their hollow semicircular bastions. *Portchester*, like *Richborough*, is rectangular. The north-west corner is now filled by the extensive remains of the medieval castle, and the south-west by the beautiful twelfth-century church of an Augustinian priory. But large though these later works are, the great expanse of the Roman fortress surrounded in the main by its original walls and towers constitutes one of our finest monuments.

There are the remains of another Saxon Shore fort at Lympne and underlying the medieval castle of *Carisbrooke* in the Isle of Wight are the walls of a rectangular fort probably also of late Roman date. At Dover an officer under the Count was stationed, but no trace of a fort has been identified. There is, however, another Roman building there which is in our care and that is the lighthouse which served as a tower to the Saxon church of St. Mary in Castro. Till the eighteenth century another similar tower stood on the western side of the harbour, but it fell into ruin. (It appears that the western lighthouse was contemporary with the Saxon Shore system, but the existing one may well be much earlier, probably late first century.)

Two other monuments of the Roman period are in the guardianship of the Ministry: the small temple on *Jordan Hill*, Weymouth, and the similar temple within the great Iron Age fort of *Maiden Castle*. Both were of a type known as "Romano-Celtic" which is commonly found in both Gaul and in Britain. That at *Maiden Castle* had a priest's house adjacent and is of interest as it was completed not earlier than 367, and was repaired later than 379. The *Jordan Hill* temple was unscientifically excavated in 1843, and it is not now possible to assign a definite date to it, but the presumption from the coins and pottery found is that it also was occupied in the later years of the fourth century. This recrudescence of paganism in the last years of official Roman rule, and at *Maiden Castle* the re-use of a prehistoric earthwork for the purpose, is a most interesting phenomenon, which has a parallel at Lydney in Gloucestershire. Other examples of the "Romano-Celtic" type, which is characterized by a square central sanctuary or *cella* and a portico all round it, have been found at *Lullingstone*, *Richborough* and *Silchester*.

In 410 the usurper, Constantine III, withdrew the troops from Britain to fight for the throne of the Empire, and it is unlikely that they ever returned. The tribal divisions of Britain were told by the legitimate Emperor Honorius to make shift for themselves, and to defend their land as best they could against Pictish and Saxon invaders. That they held out for over a century with no help from outside, and went down fighting, speaks well for the vitality of Roman culture in Britain.

Our knowledge of fifth- and even sixth-century England derivable from written records is sparse though we obtain from excavation of Saxon cemeteries some information of the kind available for the prehistoric period. We do not get back to any real certainty until the arrival of the Christian missionaries both from Papal Rome and from Ireland and Wales at the end of the sixth century, and that is the beginning of our medieval, rather than the continuance of our Roman, past.

Plate 5. Richborough Castle

Plate 6. Portchester Castle

Plate 7. Pevensey Castle

Plate 8. Old Sarum

MEDIEVAL PERIOD

Up to this point it has been possible to relate the monuments to brief historical surveys, but henceforth it will be more convenient to depart from this plan. The strands of history have become more complex and less dependent upon archæological evidence, and the monuments themselves often show modifications over a period of four or five centuries.

The medieval monuments will therefore be dealt with in two main divisions—the Anglo-Saxon period, and the period from the Norman Conquest, and instead of a history illustrated by the archæological remains, only so much historical introduction will be given as is necessary to an understanding of the individual monuments referred to in this survey.

Anglo-Saxon Period

THE Saxon settlement south of the Thames emerged in history as the kingdoms of Kent, Sussex and Wessex. When the missionaries arrived from Rome, Wessex had not reached anything like its full extent. Its northern frontier was fluid and it has been suggested that Wansdyke, a great linear earthwork reaching from the Bristol Channel to the neighbourhood of Hungerford in Berkshire, was the work of the vigorous early West Saxon King Ceawlin, to defend this frontier. It is a tradition of frontier works reaching back to the Roman Wall, through Bokerley Dyke, also in Wessex, made in the late fourth century, perhaps during the great Pictish invasion of A.D. 367 and continued in the eighth century by Offa's Dyke, against the Welsh. On the Western Marches of Wessex Roman-Celtic culture continued as far east as Dorset and Somerset, while in Cornwall and the greater part of Devon it lingered until King Egbert harried the county early in the ninth century—later still, even, for "*King Doniert's Stone*", a granite cross-shaft near St. Cleer, ornamented with interlaced patterns in the Saxon manner, but itself in a Celtic tradition of inscribed monuments, is believed to commemorate Durngarth, King of Cornwall, who was drowned in the River Fowey about 870. An earlier inscribed monument is thought to commemorate that very Tristan whose story has been incorporated in the legend of Arthur, and it was in Cornwall, the one part of southern Britain that was not overrun by the invader, that the memory of this, perhaps basically historical, hero of British resistance to the Saxons was particularly venerated. As in the Bronze Age, Cornwall asserted her links with Ireland and Brittany.

On the exposed promontory of *Tintagel* in Cornwall stand the ruins of a twelfth- and thirteenth-century castle, but excavation has proved that long before these constructions the site was occupied by a Celtic monastic settlement, which was founded about 500 A.D. and lasted until the middle of the ninth century. This romantic site is now in the guardianship of the Ministry, and though it has no authentic connection with Arthur, the remains of the early Celtic monastery are of the greatest interest.

At the other end of our region—in eastern Kent—the Ministry is guardian of three monuments of this period witnessing the earliest developments of Christianity among the Saxons. During the sixth and seventh centuries the culture of Kent was a thing apart from that of the rest of England. The magnificent jewellery and other objects found in cemeteries of Saxon period there attest the superiority in design and craftsmanship of the dwellers in east Kent over those in other parts of England at that time. The Kingdom of Kent, though it covered only east Kent, was the richest and perhaps the most populous of the southern kingdoms. The most basic reason for its position as the teacher of the rest of England in the graces of life, the arts of government and the practice of Christianity, lies in the abiding connection between its culture and the still partly Roman culture of the Merovingian Franks. It was after the Frankish pattern that the unbroken series of the English coinage began in Kent in the seventh century.

Ethelbert, King of Kent, married the daughter of Caribert, king of the region about Paris, and was recognized as overlord of all the Anglo-Saxon kingdoms south of the Humber. Soon after this marriage with a Christian princess he erected for her the church of St. Martin on the eastern outskirts of Canterbury, where in 597 he was himself baptized by the Roman missionary St. Augustine. Possibly something of his church remains in the present, certainly very ancient fabric.

Close to this church of St. Martin, on the ground which was later covered by the Norman *Abbey Church of St. Augustine*, are the remains of three churches dedicated to SS. Peter and Paul, to Our Lady and to St. Pancras, all dating from the early seventh century. In the first of these three, excavation has revealed the empty tombs of six of the first Archbishops of Canterbury, and of several Kentish kings. Shortly before the Norman Conquest the Saxon Abbot Wulfric pulled down parts of the first two churches, and began to build a great rotunda to join them into a single church. The first Norman abbot swept all this away and built a church of usual plan over the Saxon foundations. These foundations have been excavated and their plan has been laid out on the ground.

Visible from a great distance stand the gaunt twin towers of *Reculver Church*, built inside the Roman Shore fort at the mouth of the Wantsum, through which ships could sail as late as Tudor times between Thanet and the mainland of Kent. These two towers are the sad remnants of a minster church, founded by Egbert, King of Kent, in 669 and added to in the twelfth and thirteenth centuries, the greater part of which was wantonly destroyed by the deliberate action of the then vicar and his church-wardens in 1809. The late Norman towers were saved by Trinity House on account of their value as beacons for mariners. They are now looked after by the Ministry and the foundations of the Saxon church are exposed. The nave was separated from the chancel by an arcade resting on two lofty stone columns now preserved in the crypt of Canterbury Cathedral. As in the churches of Canterbury, there is much use of Roman brick and a somewhat similar floor finished in pink mortar in the Roman tradition. A notable feature of the church was a great stone cross which stood in front of the arcade on the original emplacement of the altar. The Tudor antiquary, Leland, saw it complete, its cylindrical shaft carved with bold figures of Christ and the Apostles. Some fragments of this fine sculpture may also be seen in the crypt of Canterbury Cathedral. Recent opinion has favoured a date early in the ninth century for this—the only early sculpture in the south of England that can rank in excellence with the great Anglian crosses of Bewcastle in Cumberland and Ruthwell in Dumfriesshire, a century earlier.

Very fragmentary remains of another Saxon church stand within the walls of the Roman Saxon Shore fort of *Richborough*. *Richborough* is the traditional site of the landing of St. Augustine in 597, and the chapel was probably erected to commemorate that important event, at a time when the tradition had become well-established. A stone reputed to bear the impression of St. Augustine's foot, made when he stepped on shore, was kept in the chapel, which in consequence was much frequented by pilgrims until the sixteenth century.

To the last century before the Norman Conquest belongs the massive, central-towered *Church of St. Mary in Castro*, i.e., within the castle of *Dover*. Though largely built of re-used Roman materials, it is among the grandest specimens of a style deriving from the emergent medieval architecture of the Carolingian empire, and quite different from the tenuous sub-Roman building of the missionary period. In the seventeenth century it became desecrated, and was used as a barrack store, but it was restored by Sir Gilbert Scott in 1860 and later tastelessly redecorated.

Post-Norman Conquest

OUR medieval monuments, from the Norman Conquest to the Renaissance, can be most conveniently treated by subdivision into ecclesiastical and secular buildings.

1. ECCLESIASTICAL BUILDINGS

WHEN compared with remoter and less populous regions, the southern counties are poor in conventual buildings. In this district monastic churches were either, like Romsey, Christchurch, Sherborne, and Malmesbury, converted into parish churches, or ruthlessly destroyed.

There are only seven religious houses in the southern counties of which extensive remains are in our guardianship, though we have a few other small buildings which were connected with monastic foundations and which will be included under this head. The beautiful little Norman priory church of Portchester, though within the walls of the Roman fort, is not in our care, since it is the parish church.

As has been seen at *Tintagel*, monastic communities existed in the old Celtic Church, which kept Christianity alive where the Saxons exterminated it where they settled, and in the north of England similar institutions were established under the influence of the Celtic missionaries from Iona. But in the south of England the rule of St. Benedict was introduced almost immediately by the missionaries from Rome. It flourished intermittently until the great monastic revival of the late tenth century, when many houses were founded or refounded. Most of the richest Benedictine foundations were in existence before the Norman Conquest, which, however, completely transformed them all and added many others.

The Saxon *Abbey of St. Augustine* at *Canterbury* has already been mentioned. Here as elsewhere the Normans superimposed over the Saxon foundations a far more grandiose structure. Only fragments of the great church remain above ground, though a fine Romanesque tower stood until early last century, but the large apsidal crypt, comparable to that of the neighbouring cathedral, is largely preserved except for its vault, and the radiating chapels still have painted plaster on their walls. The plan of the cloister and monastic buildings has been recovered by excavation and is partly exposed.

Another Benedictine house in our guardianship which dates originally from Saxon times is *Muchelney Abbey* in Somerset, near Langport (Plate 17). It stands on what is really an island in Sedgemoor and, in time of flood is still liable to be cut off from all communication by land. According to one tradition it was founded by King Athelstan, but there is evidence that it is a good deal older, and the original foundation may possibly be ascribed to the pious King Ine of Wessex (688–726). East of the piers of the crossing of the Norman church remains of an earlier church, carefully constructed of lias stone with semicircular apse, and a polygonal external face have been discovered. This building was first thought to have been of very early date, but it now appears that it was the immediate and perhaps unfinished predecessor of the Norman church of about 1100, which was considerably larger, though the house was never of great wealth or importance. In the fifteenth century the Norman apse was destroyed and a new and longer presbytery erected. The main portions now standing consist of the reredorter, which stands by itself, and a block comprising the south walk of the cloister, part of the frater, the kitchen, and the abbot's lodging. These buildings in their present form date from the late fifteenth and early sixteenth centuries, and contain some magnificent work of that period. After the Dissolution the abbot's lodging was used as a dwelling-house, and the other buildings fell steadily into decay.

Early in the twelfth century new Orders arose and spread rapidly; their purpose was to return to the ancient austerity of monasticism, which they felt had been corrupted by too much involvement in worldly affairs. Thus the Cistercian Order was a reassertion of the Benedictine discipline and the Premonstratensian of the milder rule of the Augustinian Canons Regular. The buildings of these Orders were usually isolated and so stand a better chance of being preserved. They are numerous in the north and west, and even in the south there are five of them in our guardianship.

Of these *Waverley Abbey* in Surrey, not yet open to the public, is important as having been the very first Cistercian house in the British Isles, founded in 1128; though not nearly as rich as the great houses of the north. The simple plan of the earliest church has been excavated: this was replaced in the thirteenth century by a large one, of the typical English Cistercian plan with a square east end. All that remains above ground are other buildings of this period, especially the vaulted lay-brothers' frater. The setting is wooded, picturesque but damp and unhealthy.

Cleeve Abbey in Somerset, founded towards the close of the twelfth century by William de Roumara, third Earl of Lincoln, as a daughter house of Revesby in Lincolnshire. This typifies the wide connections of the cosmopolitan Cistercian order. Its claustral buildings are the most complete to be seen in England, the east and south ranges retaining their roofs and floors; but the typical Cistercian church is reduced to foundations. The refectory, with a fine timber roof, was rebuilt in the later Middle Ages on the normal Benedictine plan as a first-floor hall parallel to the south alley of the cloister, and replaced an earlier refectory built at right angles to the cloister in the usual Cistercian manner. The buildings contain some notable floor-tiles and wall-paintings. The gate-house was rebuilt by the last abbot, William Dovell, who surrendered the abbey in 1537.

Netley Abbey (Plate 18) on Southampton Water was founded in 1239 and one of the latest Cistercian foundations: a daughter of the royal abbey of Beaulieu across the water, the patronage was assumed by King Henry III, though the original founder was Peter des Roches, Bishop of Winchester. Though not of the first rank as regards size, it is very complete, and of quite exceptional beauty. The ruins are extensive, and the walls of the church and of the greater part of the conventual buildings are still standing. Although so late in date, the orthodox ground plan of the Order was adhered to in the main, though with some modifications which had already been found desirable in earlier houses. At *Netley*, except for some Tudor alterations made after the Dissolution, practically all existing structures date from the middle of the thirteenth century, and few purer or more refined examples of the Early English style at its best remain to us.

Within a few miles of *Netley* are the remains of *Titchfield Abbey*, a house of Premonstratensian Canons (Plate 16) founded in 1232 also by Peter des Roches. The church was consecrated in 1238. At the Dissolution in 1537 it was given by Henry VIII to Thomas Wriothesley, Earl of Southampton, who immediately began to transform the abbey into a mansion for himself. As at *Netley*, the buildings, apart from the Tudor alterations, are pure Early English. It was to *Titchfield* that Charles I fled from *Hampton Court* in 1647, and there he was taken in custody by

Colonel Hammond, and thence conveyed to *Carisbrooke Castle*. Of the thirteenth-century church only the nave has survived Wriothesley's alterations and subsequent demolitions. The cloister, which was on the north side, became the courtyard of "Place House", as the mansion was called, the refectory became the hall and the nave the south wing. It was cut through the middle to form the great gate of the mansion; turrets were added, and Tudor windows and fireplaces inserted in the nave walls. The nave thus transformed is now almost the only part standing to full height, but many fine tiles from the paving of the cloister walks may still be seen *in situ*.

Another Premonstratensian house which has recently come into the guardianship of the Ministry is *Bayham Abbey*, on the Kent–Sussex border. It was formed early in the thirteenth century by the amalgamation of two older monasteries and ranked as a daughter house of Prémontré the mother of the whole Order. As at *Titchfield*, the nave was aisleless, but the eastern arm, which even at *Titchfield* the foundations show to have been quite complicated, at *Bayham* reached an unusual size and elaboration due to a rebuilding in the later thirteenth century. Both the church and all three ranges of claustral buildings are much better preserved than at *Titchfield*. By reason of its own qualities and its idyllic setting, *Bayham* is one of the finest monastic ruins in the south of England.

The great Benedictine Abbey of Glastonbury, one of the holiest spots in the land, where according to the legend St. Joseph of Arimathea first preached the Christian faith in Britain in the first century, is now again in the charge of the Church of England, but two small buildings which were once the property of the abbey are in the guardianship of the Ministry. One of these is the *Tribunal* or Court House. The front, with a long window extending the full width of the ground-floor room and above it a characteristic bay window below a cornice and plain parapet, was rebuilt by Abbot Bere between 1493 and 1524. Over the entrance are panels containing the Royal arms and a Tudor rose. The fine oak roofs have been restored.

The other of these buildings is the *"Fish House"* not very far distant at Meare. It was probably built in the second quarter of

Plate 9. Dover Castle

Plate 10. Dover Castle, Upper Chapel in Keep

Plate 11. Carisbrooke Castle

Plate 12. Restormel Castle

the fourteenth century for the abbey official in charge of the fishponds. It is a plain, rectangular structure of two storeys.

At *Abbotsbury* in south Dorset the Ministry has care of the small and beautifully-vaulted chapel, conspicuous on the hill-top, which, like so many other hill-tops in the country, is dedicated to St. Catherine. It is of fifteenth-century date and was probably served by the adjacent abbey which, save for its great barn nearby, has almost entirely disappeared. The gable-end of one of the monastic buildings, however, still stands, and is in the guardianship of the Ministry, while the footings of the north wall of the abbey church may be seen in the churchyard of the adjacent parish church. The two churches were side by side, as at *Muchelney*.

Another building with monastic connections and now in the charge of the Ministry is the great *barn* at Barton Farm on the outskirts of *Bradford-on-Avon*. It was built in the fourteenth century for Shaftesbury Abbey and is 174 feet long, with four porches and a most remarkable timber roof of fourteen bays. It is among the finest purely functional medieval buildings in the country and may be compared and contrasted with the equally magnificent and slightly earlier aisled barn built for Beaulieu Abbey at Great Coxwell, Berkshire, a property of the National Trust.

The Ministry also has in its guardianship two buildings in the southern counties that formerly belonged to the Order of Knights Templars. On the Western Heights at *Dover* are the foundations of the circular nave of a small twelfth-century church, the glass of which the Templars adopted in imitation of the form of the church of the Holy Sepulchre in Jerusalem; of other examples belonging to them in England the finest is the Temple Church in London. The other building associated with the Knights Templars is also in Kent, where the first-floor chamber on an undercroft of the domain of Strood Temple, still called *Temple Manor*, at *Rochester*, has survived, incorporated in later buildings.

In addition to these monuments that once belonged to the Monastic and Military Orders, four other ecclesiastical buildings are maintained by the Ministry in this area. The earliest in date

is the *Garrison Church* at *Portsmouth* which, although considerably
altered and much restored, was originally a thirteenth-century
hospital dedicated to St. John the Baptist and St. Nicholas.
This hospital was yet another of the many foundations of Bishop
Peter des Roches. The vaulted chancel of three bays, originally
the hospital chapel, is of great architectural interest and dates
from the thirteenth century. It fortunately escaped destruction
when the heavily restored nave was badly damaged by enemy
action in 1941. Charles II was married to Catherine of Braganza
in this church on May 21st, 1662. Of the once important hospital
of *Maison Dieu, Ospringe*, near Faversham, of which Henry III
ranked as founder, all trace of the religious buildings has gone.
The building in our guardianship is essentially domestic and
treated in the section on Houses.

Horne's Place Chapel, Appledore, is a fourteenth-century chapel
over an undercroft, once forming part of the building of a
manor-house. In Cornwall, *Dupath Well Chapel* is an example of
a late medieval well-house built over a holy well.

No less ecclesiastical, because all acts of public welfare were
then undertaken as acts of worship, is the tower of *St. Catherine's
Chapel* at *Chale*, Isle of Wight. The body of the chapel has
disappeared, but the tower which was a lighthouse, tended by
its priest, remains. The turret of the *Abbotsbury* chapel served a
like purpose.

2. SECULAR BUILDINGS

(i) *Castles*

THE castle and other fortifications in the southern counties which
are maintained by the Ministry are numerous and varied, but
there are none that can be compared with the castles of Wales,
planned as units during the finest period of medieval fortifications. For convenience they are treated in three groups according
to their initial date, namely, Norman, late Fourteenth Century,
and Tudor, and are dealt with under those heads.

(a) *Norman*

In *Old Sarum, i.e.* Old Salisbury (Plate 8) we have a monument of exceptional scale and interest. It is a fortified city, not merely a castle. There can be little doubt that the hill was occupied in the Iron Age and, like the rather similar hill-fort of Badbury Rings, it stands near the junction of several Roman roads. It became an important Saxon borough because it could be defended when its neighbour and rival, Wilton, was exposed to sacking by the Danes.

After harrying the north, William the Conqueror assembled his armies at *Old Sarum* in 1070 and disbanded them there. Before 1078 he transferred thither the Saxon bishopric of Sherborne. From this time date the vast earthworks as we see them to-day, transforming the Iron Age hill-fort into a citadel. The first Norman cathedral was completed by Bishop St. Osmund in 1092. It was situated in the north-western corner of the fortification where its foundations are visible. Originally apsidal, it was considerably enlarged and given a square east end by Bishop Roger who died in 1139, having completed the great tower of the castle which stands at the centre of the citadel. As long as the Bishop was in charge of castle, cathedral, and city alike, all was well. But when Henry II assumed control of the castle, and appointed his own castellan, friction between the military and ecclesiastical authorities developed. In 1217 the Dean and Chapter petitioned the Pope to inquire into their grievances. The outcome was the foundation in 1220 of the present cathedral of "new" Salisbury. In 1227 the old cathedral was finally abandoned, and thereafter used as a quarry for buildings in the new city. Many of the stones from *Old Sarum* can still be seen built into the wall round the close. The castle fell into gradual disuse and decay, and in 1446–47 is described as no longer of any value. With the abandonment of the castle, the last inhabitants left for the new city. But for many generations, until the Reform Act of 1832, though without a house or inhabitant, it continued to send two members to the House of Commons by virtue of its status as a Borough. It was perhaps the rottenest of the famous rotten boroughs, but its story is redeemed by the fact that it sent to Parliament William Pitt, afterwards the great Earl of Chatham.

Another castle of the Bishops of Salisbury, to which, unlike

Sarum, they successfully asserted their claim in the later Middle Ages was *Sherborne*, near the former seat of their bishopric. This is also in our guardianship. Here again the shaping hand was that of the great Bishop Roger, and most of the surviving work is of the Norman period, though complicated by enigmatic later alterations, some of the time of Sir Walter Raleigh. There is an extensive polygonal curtain wall with two gateways, and near the centre, the episcopal palace with a keep, or large angle tower. This shows the advanced and commodious plan, formed round a square courtyard, seen also at *Old Sarum*, and on a wider scale at the castles founded by Henry of Blois, brother of King Stephen and Bishop of Winchester from 1129, at *Wolvesey* and *Bishop's Waltham*, both as forward-looking in detail as they are in plan. For these see the end of this section.

Old Sarum is quite exceptional. More representative of a class, which was of necessity not numerous, are the great and complex fortresses of royal foundation, and dominated by a great tower or "keep".

The grandest and most mature Norman keep in the guardianship of the Ministry in the southern counties is that of *Dover Castle* (Plate 9). It is exceeded in size only by the White Tower of the *Tower of London* and the keep at Colchester, and with the possible exception of the former there is no finer or better preserved example of a square Norman keep with all its elaborations of internal planning. The keep, nearly 100 feet square and 95 feet high, was built by Henry II between 1181 and 1187. The walls are of exceptional thickness—some 22 feet at the base—and in the thickness of the walls are an unusually large number of mural chambers. The great staircase leading up to the main entrance is protected by a forebuilding which contains, near the entrance doorway into the keep and again on the next storey, two superimposed chapels (Plate 10) very richly ornamented with late Norman mouldings. In the keep is a well from the head of which a number of lead pipes carried the water to various rooms throughout the building, an unusual arrangement at this early date. The inner line of ramparts and towers was constructed immediately after the keep while the fine and very long outer line, begun at the same time, was completed in two phases in the thirteenth century, the later considerably modifying the work of the earlier. The Constable's Tower, or main gatehouse, is a fine example of military architecture of the end of that century, replacing a gatehouse at the north-west that proved to be over-exposed during the French siege of 1216.

Dover is one of the Cinque Ports, famous in medieval history as being required to furnish ships for the king for the defence of the realm. The other four original Cinque Ports were Hastings, Sandwich, Hythe, and New Romney. To these Rye and Winchelsea were added in the thirteenth century. Sandwich, Rye, and Winchelsea still preserve much of their charming medieval character. In more recent centuries the Lord Warden of the Cinque Ports, who has combined with this ancient office the Constableship of *Dover Castle*, has been either a member of the Royal Family, or a distinguished statesman, admiral, or general. His official residence is *Walmer Castle*, referred to later.

Hardly less impressive, though not on a hill-top, is the rather earlier keep of *Rochester Castle*, 125 feet high and complete to its parapet. It was built by Archbishop William of Corbeil in the 1130s and the only serious alteration is the replacement of one of the square corner turrets by a round one after it had been mined by King John's engineers in 1215 when a party of insurgent barons were holding out in the castle. The walls are less thick than those at *Dover* and the mural chambers are simpler, but the general design is advanced for its date. The entrance, protected by a forebuilding, leads into a storey which stands above two tiers of undercrofts but is still below the main hall. As at *Dover*, the forebuilding contains a chapel and the whole great tower is divided into two compartments throughout its height. The keep is not the oldest part of the castle: a single curtain wall round the bailey incorporates part of the enclosure built by Bishop Gundulf before 1100 and has a series of later towers towards the city, but the main gatehouse no longer exists.

Reference has already been made to the Norman castles formed by dividing off part of the Roman fortresses of *Portchester* and *Pevensey*.

At *Portchester* (Plate 6) the great Norman keep built at the north-west corner of the Roman fort was erected in two stages in the early and mid-twelfth century. It is only 40 feet square but looks very impressive and is an admirable example of a large but relatively simple Norman keep, beside which *Dover* shows the complexity attained in the planning of square keeps just as they were becoming outdated. Like the two foregoing it is divided into two compartments from top to bottom. *Portchester* was for long a royal castle, with a Constable appointed by the Sovereign. The walls of the inner bailey enclosing the keep were also the work of the twelfth century, but the domestic buildings put up against these walls, and the elaborate extensions of the gatehouses, are mostly work of the fourteenth century (see the section on Houses).

The keep at *Pevensey* is very ruinous but unique in type. Instead of the usual square Norman keep, we find an irregularly planned structure with several apsidal projections or bastions. It dates from around 1100. The gatehouse, walls and bastions of the inner bailey are of the first half of the thirteenth century and are in the fully developed style of that period.

Smaller in scale than these keeps, but of particular interest because of its very early date, is the keep-like tower once attached to the church of St. Leonard at *West Malling* in Kent, said to have been built by Bishop Gundolf of Rochester (1077–1108) who was also responsible for the building of the *White Tower* in London.

At *Eynsford* in Kent the Ministry is guardian of a castle which has associations with William of Eynsford, who was involved in a dispute over presentation with Archbishop Thomas Becket. The castle is of early twelfth-century date, and consists of a ditch and a tall curtain wall of flint, without towers, enclosing a polygonal area in which stand the ruins of a rectangular stone hall which resembles a keep in some features but is not, in form, a tower. It was repaired after a fire about the middle of the thirteenth century, and abandoned and dismantled early in the fourteenth.

The next group of Norman castles do not have great towers but are basically earthwork castles, with a mound or "mottee", often surmounted by a low, circular "shell" keep.

Of all the castles in the guardianship of the Ministry in the southern counties none is more frequented by visitors than *Carisbrooke* (Plate 11) in the Isle of Wight. Its association with Charles I, who was imprisoned in its walls by the victorious Parliamentarian forces, has made it an object of pilgrimage. But, apart from its historic associations, it is one of the most interesting of all our national monuments from an archæological point of view.

On all sides of the great Norman bailey we can still trace the remains of the Roman fort that occupied the site. At the Norman Conquest the Isle of Wight was granted to William FitzOsbern, and doubtless the large Norman earthwork—motte and the great banks round the bailey—was his work or that of his son. From 1107 onwards the island was held by the powerful baronial House of Redvers who built the existing circular or "shell" keep on the older motte, and enclosed the bailey with a curtain wall, much of which still stands. This type of castle, where the keep is of "shell" type on a motte, as distinct from a great tower on level ground, will be observed in many of the following examples.

The Countess Isabella, daughter of Baldwin de Redvers IV, and widow of William de Fortibus, was the last of her line. She held the castle from 1263 to 1292, and to her we owe the rebuilding of much of the Great Hall, the adjoining Chapel of St. Peter and two chambers. At the Countess's death the castle was sold to the Crown.

The twin-towered gatehouse, still the entrance to the castle, was added in 1335–36. Towards the end of the fourteenth century the Earl of Salisbury, who then held the castle on the king's behalf, added to the domestic buildings which were further modified in the fifteenth and, particularly, the sixteenth centuries.

Finally, between 1597 and 1600, new and very much larger lines of defence were made in the Italian manner of artillery fortification, enclosing the whole of the old castle. This work, by far the best example of its type in the region, is discussed below. In modern time the domestic buildings have been somewhat drastically restored, and the chapel of St. Nicholas rebuilt from its foundations. The Governor's apartments now house the museum.

The same House of Redvers that held *Carisbrooke* also held the hundred and castle of *Christchurch*, or Twineham, on the mainland opposite the western end of the Island and were patrons of the Augustinian prior there. Of their castle both the motte, somewhat altered in shape and surmounted by a post-Norman keep, and the hall or *Norman House* are in the guardianship of the Ministry. The latter is described in more detail below (under Houses).

The keep of *Farnham Castle* in Surrey was placed under our guardianship by the Bishop of Guildford shortly after that diocese had been carved out of the ancient diocese of Winchester. The castle had remained a residence of the Bishops of Winchester until 1927. The great earthen motte was originally surmounted by a central tower, of which the deep foundations, built up with the motte, have been excavated. This was a work of the early part of the episcopate of the ambitious Bishop Henry of Blois, brother of King Stephen, who also built the triangular bailey in which is the Bishop's hall and was the founder of the fortified palaces of *Wolvesey* and *Bishop's Waltham*. Probably after the tower had been thrown down by order of Henry II, either Bishop Henry or his immediate successors began the huge shell-keep which now surrounds the motte. The conspicuous corner-tower of the bailey was built by Bishop Waynflete in the late fifteenth century, and the surviving additions to the entrance to the keep date from the time of Bishop Fox (1500–28).

The castle fell into the hands of the French in 1216, but was recaptured next year by the Earl of Pembroke. During the Civil War it changed hands twice, and under Cromwell's rule it was confiscated; but at the Restoration it was given back to the Bishop of Winchester.

Ludgershall Castle, on the road from Andover to Marlborough, is maintained by the Ministry, as it is on Ministry of Defence property. The earliest record of it in history is in 1141, when the Empress Maud took refuge within its walls. It was a royal castle, and throughout the thirteenth century the King appointed governors who were generally in charge of Marlborough Castle as well. Edward II, however, seems to have appointed no governors, and the castle fell into decay. In 1540 it was described as "clene down", but there are quite extensive ruins, now much more intelligible after excavation, and formidable earthworks of motte-and-bailey plan.

In 1337 Edward III made his eldest son, the Black Prince, Duke of Cornwall and thereafter the lands of the Duchy of Cornwall have always been an apanage of the eldest son of the reigning Sovereign. Edward VIII when Prince of Wales placed three castles of the Duchy under our guardianship.

The smallest of these is *Lydford* in Devon. This looks like an earthwork castle of the usual motte and bailey type, but most of the apparent motte was banked up against the rectangular stone tower-house of three storeys erected in 1195 specifically as a prison. It was modified about 1260 by Richard, Earl of Cornwall, the younger brother of Henry III, who was chosen by the German Electors as King of the Romans but never attained the full dignity of Holy Roman Emperor, to which his ambitions aspired. It was of little military importance, but continued in use as a prison, while on the upper floor the Stannary Court, or court of the tin mines, of the neighbourhood met. This court earned an unenviable reputation for severity—and Browne, the local seventeenth-century poet, wrote:

> "I oft have heard of Lydford Law
> How in the morn they hang and draw
> And sit in judgment after."

The second of these Duchy castles, also of Norman origin is *Restormel* (Plate 12), about 1½ miles from Lostwithiel. The circular motte upon which the castle now stands was erected almost certainly about 1100 by Baldwin Fitz Turstin, the Sheriff of Cornwall. The masonry gate may also be of early date, but the shell-keep (125 feet in diameter) dates from about 1200, and rooms and other buildings within it were built probably by Edmund, son of Richard, Earl of Cornwall, at the end of the thirteenth century. To this date belongs also the rectangular chapel projected outwards from the keep. The Black Prince is known to have visited this castle in 1365. It was garrisoned and fought for in the Civil War, being captured by Sir Richard Grenville in 1644, an episode which closes its history. It forms

D

to-day one of the most attractive of our ancient monuments in its woodland setting.

Reference has already been made to the Celtic monastery at *Tintagel* in Cornwall. The name Tintagel first occurs in that famous "history" of Geoffrey of Monmouth in the twelfth century, which clothed the obscure legends of King Arthur and the Knights of the Round Table with the romance of later medieval chivalry. The name is not Celtic but Norman-French, and its most romantic and impressive situation may have inspired Geoffrey's gifts as a writer of fiction. The castle was, in fact, first built by Reginald, Earl of Cornwall, an illegitimate son of Henry I who held *Tintagel* and other lands of the earldom from 1140 to 1175.

The visible remains were mostly built between 1236 and 1272 under Richard, Earl of Cornwall (see under *Lydford*). The castle fell into disrepair as early as the fourteenth century. The narrow cliff-girt site is in itself a formidable fortress, but its weather-beaten masonry walls, while adding to the picturesqueness of the scene, are of no special architectural quality.

Three other West-Country castles of this period, which have been placed in the guardianship of the Ministry, remain to be mentioned. Very similar to *Restormel* is the well preserved shell-keep of *Totnes Castle*, in Devon, standing on the summit of a hill above the borough of that name. Together with the stone curtain walls, it was first built early in the thirteenth century on the earthworks of a motte and bailey castle that had been erected by Judhael in the time of William I. In the early fourteenth century its walls were reconstructed, but the plan of the earlier work was followed.

Launceston Castle, in Cornwall, known throughout the Middle Ages as Dunheved, was the principal seat of Robert of Mortain, brother of the Conqueror, who also held *Pevensey*. The present stone defences, however, which include inner and outer wards with curtain walls, and a keep on a high motte, are mainly of the twelfth and thirteenth centuries. The keep is of particular interest, and has points of similarity with the later structure at *Flint* in North Wales. It consists of a cylindrical tower surrounded by a concentric curtain wall, the ground-floor space between the two being originally roofed over. As at *Carisbrooke*, it was approached by a steep stairway up the face of the mound.

The castle of *Okehampton*, though of Norman origin, was largely rebuilt soon after 1300. Its site on a ridge leading up to a steep knoll provided a ready-made motte-and-bailey plan that needed little artificial improvement, the natural bailey being long and narrow. It makes the most of a rocky and restricted site, reminiscent of German hill-top castles and shares something of their picturesqueness.

In quite a different category from these mounded fortresses are the two fortified palaces of the Bishops of Winchester, at *Wolvesey*, just without the city and *Bishop's Waltham*, some miles to the east. *Wolvesey* still belongs to the Bishop, who has his seventeenth-century palace next door: *Waltham* was finally forfeited after being sacked, like Farnham, in the Civil War. Both occupy a broad and level moated site, with the buildings ranged round an extensive quadrangle, and both have a principal tower which can be regarded as a "keep", but the accent is on the provision of space and dignity in a long suite of great halls and chambers on the upper floor, rather than sheer martial strength, and this development is carried further than at *Old Sarum* or *Sherborne*. They foreshadow, in the Norman period, the palatial accommodation of the later castles described in the next section. At *Bishop's Waltham* the Norman buildings have been much reconstructed in later periods, particularly under Bishop Langton in the 1490s, but the Romanesque apsidal crypt of the chapel remains; at *Wolvesey* the late medieval chapel is incorporated in the present palace.

(b) Fourteenth Century

In the southern counties there are four castles of the late fourteenth century in our guardianship. There is a considerable group of these castles in the country, and they represent a distinct stage in the transition from the Norman fortress to the Tudor mansion. They are rather fortified residences than castles proper, and though they largely follow the form of their proto-type in still providing for defence, in their internal arrangements they devote more attention to the amenities of civilized life.

The earliest of these is *Nunney Castle* in east Somerset (Plate 13) which was built by John de la Mare, who obtained licence to crenellate from Edward III in 1373. It consists of a high compact rectangle with round angle towers, a completely French type without parallel in England, and is surrounded by a moat which has been excavated and again filled with water. It was held for the King in the Civil War, but was captured by the Parliament after a one-day siege and the interior was then dismantled. The north wall collapsed in 1910.

Not far away and of similar date is *Farleigh Castle*. Licence to crenellate was granted in 1383 to Sir Thomas Hungerford, and the castle remained for many generations the property of the Hungerford family. It is of the usual English plan, on an extensive moated site, incorporating features of a castle of earlier date. A curtain wall with round angle towers surrounds an inner ward which contains the living quarters, and in the outer ward is the chapel, originally the parish church. The castle itself fell into ruins in the eighteenth century, but the chapel is roofed, and contains some fine tombs of the Hungerfords, a fifteenth-century iron grille, and a Jacobean pulpit.

A rather specialized case of the same period is *Donnington Castle*, near Newbury, where the roughly quadrilateral curtain wall is quite feeble and the gatehouse of exaggerated height and strength.

Old Wardour Castle, in southern Wiltshire, is another specialized case, of great architectural refinement. It was built by John, Lord Lovel, who obtained licence to crenellate in 1392, and most of the building dates from that period. In plan it is hexagonal, surrounding a central courtyard of the same shape, and thus is unique among English castles. In 1547 it came into the possession of the Arundel family, the present owners, and after 1570 Sir Matthew Arundel made several curious additions and alterations in the Elizabethan Renaissance style (Plate 19). In the Civil War it was besieged first by the Parliament and then by the Royalists, and during the second siege the whole western wing was blown up, since when the castle has remained a ruin. It is in a lovely setting and was preserved as a picturesque feature in a park of the newer Wardour Castle, which was built in 1776 to the design of James Paine.

Perhaps the best-known of this late fourteenth-century group is Bodiam, a property of the National Trust, but *Hurstmonceux*, a similar though early fifteenth-century example of brick, also in Sussex, is in the care of the Ministry. The interior, completely rebuilt, is not accessible to the public, but the exterior may be inspected at certain times. The quadrilateral plan, broad moat, angle towers and the gatehouse in the centre of the front can be well appreciated.

(c) Tudor

During the fifteenth and sixteenth centuries domestic and military architecture parted company, and developed along separate lines. The increased use of artillery rendering many of the older castles ineffective, new styles of fortification were gradually evolved, particularly for coastal defence.

One of the earliest is The Strong Tower, now known as *Dartmouth Castle* (Plate 14). This does not strictly belong to the Tudor period but may be included here, since it has greater affinity with the later castles for coast defence than with the last group we have been considering. It was erected in 1481 by the Corporation of Dartmouth and provided with gun-ports from the beginning. It remains substantially as it was built, and was handed over to the then Office of Works by the War Office in 1910. In the town of Dartmouth is the slightly later blockhouse *Bayard's Cove Castle*.

The most substantial additions to the defences of the coast were made in the reign of Henry VIII. It is probable that *St. Catherine's Castle*, Fowey, and the original smaller fort at *Pendennis*, now called Little Dennis fort, should be attributed to the middle of his reign. But shortly after the Suppression of the Monasteries Henry embarked upon a comprehensive scheme of coastal defence. "Blockhouses" or "bulwarks" were proposed for every haven and at every possible landing place. Many of these were never built, but within the following few years work was proceeding upon a number of small castles and similar works along the coast from Hull to Milford Haven. Most of these are low, but very massive structures, often consisting of a central tower with larger circular bastions pierced with wide embrasures for guns.

Two of the finest, namely, *Pendennis* and *St. Mawes Castles* (Plate 15) in Cornwall, were begun in or about 1540 to defend Falmouth Haven, and are still well preserved. They illustrate the King's intention to have the defences erected in the most up-to-date style, which, however, in a few years became obsolete. Other similar blockhouse fortresses of this date in our guardianship are *Deal*, *Walmer*, *Calshot*, *Hurst* and *Portland Castles*, some of which have been much altered since their foundation, and *Yarmouth Castle*, Isle of Wight, the latest of the series, which is rectangular in plan, and with its pointed bastion prefigures a completely new theory of fortification best exemplified at *Carisbrooke* (see below).

Walmer Castle is the official residence of the Lord Warden of the Cinque Ports. It contains a small collection of historical relics and the room in which the famous Duke of Wellington (who held the office of Lord Warden) died in 1852. The contents of this room and its decoration were either the Duke's own or, as with the wall-paper and carpet, reproductions of those installed by him. As a consequence this Wellington room is an interesting and complete example of early Victorian taste.

The scheme of coastal defences was continued, under Edward VI, right down to the Scilly Isles, where *King Charles's Castle* and Harry's Walls on Tresco probably belong to this reign. The former was a two-storey, oblong fort with a semi-hexagonal western end in which gun-ports still remain, while the latter is square with bastions at the angles. The entrance doorway was at the eastern end. *Cromwell's Castle*, also on Tresco, was named after the Protector Oliver, and was constructed about 1650. The castle is a high, cylindrical tower, the upper storey of which is pierced with six gun-ports. Both this and *King Charles's Castle* were intended to protect New Grimsby Haven. But perhaps the final addition to the Henrician scheme was *Upnor Castle*, built early in the reign of Elizabeth I to protect the haven at the mouth of the Medway.

Later in the sixteenth century these masonry blockhouses became out of date, and engineers reverted once more to defences of earth. Ramparts were constructed of soil or timber, and frequently revetted with sloping walls of stone or brick. Angular bastions of various forms were added to ensure command with cross-fire over the whole of the ramparts. This system was much elaborated by the famous French engineer Vauban and others in later centuries, but some of the earliest examples of the type now to be seen in this country are the outer defences of *Carisbrooke*, which were mostly erected between 1597 and 1602, and the outer defences of *Pendennis Castle* of about 1598. The fortifications of this period were the result of the long war with Spain. The *Carisbrooke* works were erected by an Italian, Federigo Gianibelli, who also had a share in the Elizabethan defences of *Berwick-on-Tweed* and the fortifications of Antwerp; those of *Pendennis* were partly altered in the reign of Charles I and the castle was thus able to withstand a long siege during the Civil War (1646).

(ii) *Houses*

THE principal feature of the medieval English house, whether large or small, was its hall, which served not only as the living-room and dining-room of the whole household, but sometimes as a common dormitory as well. The hall was a single large room, with or without aisles, its floor either at ground-level or raised above an undercroft, and reached from the outside through a doorway set near the end of one of its side walls. It was heated by a central hearth set on the floor or else by a fireplace in one of the walls. At the opposite end to the entrance was a dais where the lord of the manor or master of the household and his family could sit overlooking their dependants who used the body of the hall. These general arrangements were common to the domestic building set within medieval castles and to the unfortified or semi-fortified manor houses of the countryside, and the characteristic keep is externally a massive fortified tower but internally a house with its hall raised on an undercroft. The earliest examples of halls, outside keeps, in the guardianship of the Ministry are those at *Eynsford* in Kent and the *Norman House* at *Christchurch* in Hampshire which, though not themselves of great strength, are the halls of castles.

The house at *Christchurch* was built about the 1160s by Richard
or Baldwin de Redvers, who were also Lords of *Carisbrooke*,
and is a two-storeyed stone building with one large room on each
floor. The ground-floor room, lighted by loops, has the remains
of a newel staircase in one corner. The hall was on the first floor
and access to it was by means of an external flight of steps which
has now gone. It had a fireplace in one wall, the fine cylindrical
chimney of which has survived, and three round-headed
windows, each of two lights, rabbeted for shutters and enriched
with chevron ornament. Besides the example at *Eynsford*, which
has two, unconnected rooms on the ground floor, one of which
was a separate lodging, there are remains of another Norman
first-floor hall house at *Portchester*, and a later instance is seen in
the abbot's house at *Netley*.

An early development from the primitive hall plan was the
addition of a private chamber or solar at the dais end for the
use of the lord and his family. An excellent example of this,
placed in the guardianship of the Ministry by the National Trust,
can be seen at *Old Soar*, near Plaxtol in Kent, where the solar
block of a manor house of the Colepepper family, built in the
last years of the thirteenth century, has survived almost intact.
The site of the ground-floor hall is now occupied by an
eighteenth-century house, but a remaining corbel shows that it
possessed aisles. The solar block consists of three rooms at
first-floor level, each standing over an undercroft and grouped at
the dais end of the hall. The largest room was the solar itself,
reached by a newel staircase and provided with window-seats, a
fireplace and a cupboard. It retains its original timber roof of
crown-post construction. From the angles project two smaller
rooms, one a garderobe, the other a chapel.

Later medieval buildings of domestic character in the guardianship of the Ministry are *Kirkham House* in *Paignton*, *Fiddleford
Mill House* in north Dorset and the *Maison Dieu* at *Ospringe*, The
first is a well-preserved fourteenth-century stone house, with
timber-framed partitions, heavy timber surrounds to the door-
and window-openings, and many features typical of West-
Country "vernacular" building; the second is the same sort of
building, but socially of rather higher status and not all under

Plate 13. Nunney Castle

Plate 14. Dartmouth Castle

Plate 15. St. Mawes Castle

Plate 16. Titchfield Abbey

one roof. Here, as at *Old Soar*, is a well-finished solar, or great chamber, but at the other end of the hall. The hall was much altered and made not only more up to date, but grander, in the sixteenth century, but both parts have very elaborate and essentially West-Country, fourteenth-century roofs. The *Maison Dieu* house is of a more urban plan; a stone fragment of an early fourteenth-century house is incorporated in a typical example of early sixteenth-century Kentish domestic timber building. It was part of the complex of a medieval hospital, but even the oldest part is purely residential in character.

The buildings of Richard II at *Portchester Castle* (see above) form a complete example of a late medieval house on a palatial scale, with great hall and other major rooms raised above undercrofts. Though bounded by the curtain-wall of the castle, they are as independent of military considerations as is the earlier house at *Christchurch*. What remains at *Eltham* is part of a major royal palace rebuilt in the following century. The great hall, at ground level, not on an undercroft, dates from the 1470s and has an outstanding hammer-beam roof, but most of the subordinate buildings have gone and the ensemble of the palace is far less complete than *Portchester*, nearly a century older. Later yet than *Eltham*, but still thoroughly medieval in plan and detail, is what remains of the "Place House" created on a princely scale by Wriothesley out of the buildings of *Titchfield Abbey* (see above).

(iii) *Roads and Bridges*

THE medieval transport system, though less centralized than the Roman, was not chaotic and in some ways mechanically more efficient. To improve it, as by building bridges and causeways (compare *St. Catherine's Chapel, Chale*, as a lighthouse) was an act of piety. Some medieval bridges, such as the fine series over the Medway and its tributaries, all scheduled as ancient monuments, are among the noblest monuments of the Middle Ages. The only one in guardianship in this area is *Gallox Bridge*, Dunster, Somerset, which is typical of many stone packhorse bridges, sturdy but too narrow for wheeled transport.

RENAISSANCE PERIOD

It might seem absurd to name a period of English architecture after a movement which had passed its climacteric in Italy over a century earlier. Nevertheless, the great Inigo Jones was the first English architect to conceive buildings radically in the Renaissance manner and not merely to incorporate Italianate elements (see *Old Wardour* above). One of the most important and seminal buildings in our charge is the *Queen's House* (Plate 20) at Greenwich, which he designed.

The old Greenwich Palace, greatly enlarged by Henry VIII, lay along the bank of the Thames. To the south lay Greenwich Park, between which and the Palace gardens ran a public road. Queen Anne of Denmark, who had been granted the Manor of Greenwich by her husband, James I, proposed to unite the Palace gardens and the park by a bridge over the road incorporated in a small Italian palace. Inigo Jones was entrusted with the design in 1616, but on the death of the Queen in 1618 the work was stopped, and then resumed under Charles I, who gave the house to Queen Henrietta Maria. We know that internal decorations were still being carried out in 1637. The old Palace was destroyed in the Civil Wars, but the new *Queen's House* was saved. At the Restoration, repairs and some alterations were made by John Webb, Inigo Jones' pupil; and Henrietta Maria, as Queen Mother, returned to live in it till her death in 1669. Thereafter it was granted in turn to Queen Catherine of Braganza and Queen Mary of Modena, but neither lived in it. After the Revolution of 1688 it was occupied by successive Rangers of Greenwich Park, who from 1710 to 1729 were the Governors of the Royal Hospital.

In 1806 the *Queen's House* was handed over to the Royal Naval Asylum, afterwards merged in the Greenwich Hospital School. It was much altered internally, and the existing stone colonnades were built on either side of the house to connect it with the new wings of the school. On the removal of the school in 1933, the *Queen's House* was placed in the charge of the then Office of Works as an ancient monument, and the worst of the later disfigurements were removed. The use of it was then granted to the National Maritime Museum, and it was opened to the public by King George VI and Queen Elizabeth in 1937. Every effort has been made to present the internal as well as external appearance of the house as nearly as possible as Jones designed them.

The entrance hall is a perfect cube of 40 feet, and retains its original ceiling (though without the paintings with which it was adorned) and projecting wooden gallery. The circular staircase with its fine ironwork balustrade is also of the period of Inigo Jones, as are the elaborate decorations of the ceilings of the two principal north rooms on the first floor. The colonnades mark the line of the public roadway which ran through the building. It was blocked in the eighteenth century, but it is still spanned by the original bridge which connected the two separate wings, and by two other bridges added by Webb in 1661.

Another former Royal residence, *Kew Palace*, is open during the summer. This red brick building originally known as "the Dutch House" was built by one Samuel Fortrey, a Dutchman, in the reign of Charles I. His initials and the date 1631 still appear in the pediment over the main doorway. It is of four storeys, and is an interesting example of the Low-Country Renaissance style of this date, which had a brief vogue in England, and of precociously compact planning. The house was acquired on lease by George II for Queen Caroline about 1730. It was later occupied by Frederick, Prince of Wales, and after his death by his widow, whose son, George III, purchased it in 1781 as a "nursery" for the numerous Royal children. Later it was occupied by Queen Charlotte, who died there in 1818. Many alterations to the windows, doors, and the interior of the house generally were carried out by Prince Frederick, between 1737 and 1748, probably under the supervision of William Kent. Some of the furniture now in the building dates back to this time, but other pieces, including the pictures, have been given or lent in recent years. They come for the most part from the Royal Collections and the Victoria and Albert Museum.

Another important building of the same period, *Ham House*, was given in 1948 by the Tollemache family to the National Trust, which leased it at a nominal rent to the Ministry of Public Building and Works. This splendid example of seventeenth-century domestic architecture began as an H-shaped house, built by Sir Thomas Vavasour, whose initials, with the date 1610, appear on the doorway of the north front. A striking feature of the latter are its loggias in the Italian style, reminiscent of those at Holland House, Kensington; another is the great staircase, with its pierced balustrade and carved trophies. The house was largely given its present form after the Restoration, when it was the home of the Duke of Lauderdale, one of the members of the notorious Cabal. In particular the south ends of the cross-wings were enlarged and were united by a range of splendid state rooms to form a new south front.

Within, the house is remarkable not only for its superb wood-work and plasterwork decoration, but for the completeness of its seventeenth-century furnishings, many of which, like the pictures in the Long Gallery, still occupy the very rooms for which they were designed, the whole presenting an unrivalled impression of the rich character of a great Baroque mansion. These fittings are in the care of the Victoria and Albert Museum.

These last two examples are in brick with detail on a relatively modest scale, as is also the *Royal Observatory* at the summit of Greenwich Park, erected in 1675–76 to the designs of the great Sir Christopher Wren with a dignity he doubtless thought proper to the mathematical sciences that were so close to his heart. There is a marked contrast between them and the severe grandeur of three stone buildings, all major works of their kind, which are also in the care of the Ministry. These date from the decades following the Restoration of Charles II when classical architecture in England came at last to maturity. The patronage that produced them was different in each case but it is historically significant that the British monarch could only with difficulty rise to the expense of such buildings as his Continental colleagues could command, while the latest of the three, Appuldurcombe though not less in splendour, is but the private house of a not particularly wealthy squire.

The greatest of these buildings is also at Greenwich. The *Royal Naval College*, formerly the Royal Naval Hospital, incorporates in the "King Charles Block" all that was achieved of that King's attempt to rebuild the Palace. The designer was Webb, who added to the *Queen's House*. In 1694 it was converted to the use of the new *Naval Hospital* and enlarged on a plan that might rival the French royal hospital for army *Invalides* in Paris. Three new blocks on the same scale were added in turn, named after King William, Queen Mary and Queen Anne respectively, and many famous architects had a hand in the scheme—Wren, his assistant Hawksmoor, Vanburgh who had even bigger ideas, Colin Campbell and Ripley. In turn they carried the construction over more than fifty years, but the unity of the whole scheme remains in the grandest architectural composition in England.

Beside *Greenwich Hospital*, *Abingdon County Hall* (begun in 1677) is small but it is a public building of a scale and dignity rare in England at any period, and the influence, if not the hand, of Wren can be felt in its composition. It is a highly sophisticated example of a type of pillared market hall, usually with a chamber over it, widely distributed in English country towns, and of which the *Dunster Yarn Market* in Somerset is an earlier and much more "vernacular" specimen. At *Appuldurcombe* in the Isle of Wight, there stands the shell of a fine house begun in a confident Baroque manner by Sir Robert Worsley in 1710 and completed by Sir Richard Worsley later in the century.

The final group of monuments to be mentioned brings us back to coastal defence and the continued development of artillery fortification which, though very much an aspect of Renaissance science, has thus far been covered in the section of medieval castles. The earliest is the plain and utilitarian defensive tower known as *Mount Batten*, or more properly *Mount Batton, Castle*, built in 1665 on an island in Plymouth roadsteads. Its name, with this ambience of English naval legend, has formed a most providential translation for that of the princely German family which has so splendidly made this tradition its own. Some, however, are more notable for their architectural pretensions and two of them are now divorced from the fortifications to which they belong. After the Restoration certain coastal forts were strengthened and the *Citadel* at *Plymouth* was constructed. Only its elaborate Gate, bearing the date 1670, and the *Statue of George II* that adorns it, are in our charge. The gate may be compared with the similar structure at *Tilbury Fort*, on the Thames, which is dated 1682 and is also in the guardianship of the Ministry. Of the same character but less elaborate are two gates at *Portsmouth*. The defences of the town (as opposed to the harbour), consisting of earthwork and ditch, were planned by Henry VIII and executed under Elizabeth I. In 1624 they were so damaged by a storm that in the years following it was proposed to remove them. They were repaired, however, by both Charles I and Cromwell, but after the Restoration a new plan was drawn up in 1665, and gradually completed, and it is to this scheme that our two gates belong. *King James's Gate* was completed in 1687, and the *Landport Gate* (also called St. George's or the Old Town Gate), which formed the principal entrance to the town from the harbour, was finished in 1698. This still stands on its original site, but *King James's Gate* was re-erected in its present position when the old defences of Portsmouth were demolished in the 1870s.

The latest of the coastal defences in the care of the Ministry are representative of the same tradition. They consist of a line of land defences behind the real defences which always lay out to sea, and which, perhaps fortunately, ensured that they were never put to the test. A *Martello Tower* at *Dymchurch*, Kent, is part of the system laid out in the Napoleonic wars along the coasts of Sussex, Kent, Essex and Suffolk and not in fact built until the danger of invasion had been averted at Trafalgar. The fortifications on the *Western Heights* at *Dover* are typical of a series of grandiose constructions which continued well into the Victorian period. They were centred around ports and naval bases, Portsmouth being the most heavily defended. No two of them are alike, but the most impressive ones make use of positions of natural strength.

NOTES

The following list of monuments in the care of the Ministry of Public Building and Works includes a brief description of each monument and information about access and admission.

Guide books are obtainable at monuments marked with a dagger (†). They may also be obtained from Her Majesty's Stationery Office at the addresses shown on the inside back cover. At a number of monuments for which guide books are not yet available, the custodians have notes of their history and plans which can be inspected without extra charge.

Postcards are on sale at monuments marked with an asterisk (*). They may also be obtained from the Clerk of Stationery, Ministry of Public Building and Works, Lafone House, 11/13 Leather-market St., London, S.E.1. (122 George Street, Edinburgh 2, for Scottish monuments.)

Photographs may be taken by visitors without a permit, except at buildings occupied by H.M. Forces, where special permission may sometimes be necessary. The use of stand cameras is subject to the discretion of the custodian.

Official Photographs of most monuments may be obtained in large prints at commercial rates from the Photographic Librarian, Ministry of Public Building and Works, Hannibal House, Elephant and Castle, London, S.E.1. (122 George Street, Edinburgh 2, for Scottish monuments.)

Admission Fees range from 3d. to 4s. Admission is free at monuments marked with a double asterisk.

Old age pensioners and children under fifteen years of age are admitted at half price. Organized parties of eleven or more can claim a discount of 10 per cent. of the total admission fee. Full payment is made on admission to the Custodian, who will supply a duplicate of a completed form to be sent within three months by the party leader to the Ministry, (Accounts 7A), Prince Consort House, Albert Embankment, London, S.E.1, when a discount will be refunded.

Season Tickets, valid for a year, admit their holders to all ancient monuments and historic buildings in the care of the Ministry of Public Building and Works. They cost 15s. (old age pensioners and children under 15, 7s. 6d.) and can be obtained by writing to the Ministry (AM/P), Lambeth Bridge House, London, S.E.1; at the H.M.S.O. bookshops listed on the inside back cover or at most monuments.

Standard Hours of Admission are:

	Weekdays	*Sundays*
March–April	9.30 a.m.—5.30 p.m.	2 p.m.—5.30 p.m.
May–September	9.30 a.m.—7 p.m.	2 p.m.—7 p.m.
October	9.30 a.m.—5.30 p.m.	2 p.m.—5.30 p.m.
November–February	10 a.m.—4.30 p.m.	2 p.m.—4.30 p.m.

Variations from the Standard Hours are noted under the particular monument.

BERKSHIRE

**†*Abingdon County Hall*

An outstanding example of a seventeenth-century public building. Built between 1677 and 1683 as a Court for the Justices of Assize and a market hall.

Situation: In Abingdon.

Hours of Admission: Standard.

**Donnington Castle, Newbury*

The castle was built towards the end of the fourteenth century, and the tower-like gatehouse of that date remains. There are extensive earthwork defences of the time of the Civil War, when the castle underwent a long siege.

Situation: 1 mile north of Newbury.

Hours of Admission: Standard.

**Uffington White Horse and Castle*

A large Iron Age camp surrounded by a rampart and a single ditch. The horse below the camp is cut in the turf and is perhaps of the same date. At the foot of the hill is the natural mound known as Dragon's Hill.

Situation: 2 miles south of Uffington.

Admission: At any time.

**Wayland's Smithy, Ashbury*

A prehistoric burial place consisting of a long earthen mound containing a cruciform chamber, formed of large blocks of stone, in which the human remains were placed.

Situation: 1 mile east of Ashbury.

Admission: At any time.

CORNWALL

†*Carn Euny Ancient Village, Sancreed*

An Iron Age village with stone houses and a fine "fogou" 60 feet long.

Situation: 1¼ miles south-west of Sancreed.

Hours of Admission: Standard.

E

†*Chysauster Ancient Village, Madron

An Iron Age village dating from the first to the third century A.D., consisting of a series of stone houses, each containing a number of rooms surrounding an open court. The walls of the excavated buildings stand several feet high.

Situation: 2½ miles north-west of Gulval.

Hours of Admission: Standard but Sundays from 9.30 a.m., April to September.

**Dupath Well Chapel, Callington

An almost complete well-house built over a holy well, *c.* 1500.

Situation: About 1 mile east of the village.

Admission: At any time.

**King Doniert's Inscribed Stone, St. Cleer

Part of a cross-shaft decorated with interlaced pattern and inscribed "DONIERT ROGAVIT PRO ANIMA". Doniert was probably the same as Durngarth, King of Cornwall in the latter half of the ninth century. There is also part of another cross-shaft with similar decoration.

Situation: 1 mile north-west of St. Cleer.

Admission: At any time.

†*Launceston Castle

A fine castle overlooking the town of Launceston. It was a seat of Robert of Mortain, brother of William I, but the present stone defences, which include inner and outer wards with curtain walls, and a cylindrical keep on the summit of a high mound, are mainly of the twelfth and thirteenth centuries. The castle was taken by the Parliamentarians in 1646 and later slighted.

Situation: In Launceston.

Hours of Admission: Standard.

†*Pendennis Castle

A well-preserved castle erected by Henry VIII for coast defence. It was enlarged by Elizabeth I. In the Civil War in 1646 it was besieged by the Parliamentary Army under General Fairfax; the siege lasted five months, the garrison capitulating and marching out with colours flying.

Situation: About 1 mile south-east of Falmouth.

Hours of Admission: Standard, but Sundays from 9.30 a.m., May to September.

†*Restormel Castle (Plate 12)

A large, interesting and picturesquely situated Norman motte-and-bailey castle, the walls on the motte forming a large shell-keep of *c.* 1200 with a slightly earlier gatehouse. The stone domestic buildings within the circumference, from the late thirteenth century onwards, probably replaced wooden buildings. No stonework remains in the bailey.

Situation: About 1½ miles north of Lostwithiel.

Hours of Admission: Standard, but Sundays from 9.30 a.m., May to September.

**St. Breock Downs, monolith

A long stone of prehistoric date originally about 16 ft. in height.

Situation: On St. Breock Downs, 3¾ miles south-south-west of Wadebridge.

Admission: At any time.

**St. Catherine's Castle, Fowey

A fort erected in the reign of Henry VIII for the defence of the harbour.

Situation: ¾ mile south-west of Fowey.

Admission: At any time.

**St. Just, Ballowall Barrow

A remarkable chambered barrow with concentric walls.

Situation: Near Carn Gloose, 1 mile west of St. Just.

Admission: At any time.

†*St. Mawes Castle (Plate 15)

A fine castle erected by Henry VIII for coast defence. It consists of a central tower with three semicircular bastions. Inscriptions in Latin verse adorn the tower and bastions.

Situation: 2 miles east of Falmouth across the estuary.

Hours of Admission: Standard, but Sundays from 9.30 a.m., May to September.

****"The Hurlers" Stone Circles, Minions**

Three prehistoric stone circles in a line; one of the best examples of this
type of monument in the south-west.

Situation: ½ mile north-west of Minions.

Admission: At any time.

†*Tintagel Castle

The remains of a medieval castle standing in a picturesque position overlooking the sea. It was built in the middle of the twelfth century by Reginald,
Earl of Cornwall, and has now been divided into two parts by the erosion
of the sea.
On the headland there are also the remains of a Celtic monastery of the fifth
to the ninth centuries, similar in type to other examples in Ireland and Wales.

Situation: ½ mile north-west of Trevena.

Hours of Admission: Standard, but Sundays from 9.30 a.m., May to
September.

****Trethevy Quoit, St. Cleer** (Plate 2)

A prehistoric burial-chamber consisting of five standing stones surmounted
by a huge capstone.

Situation: 1 mile north-east of St. Cleer.

Admission: At any time.

SCILLY ISLES

Official Guide Book. All the monuments in the Isles of Scilly
which are mentioned below are included in the guide to the
Ancient Monuments of the Isles of Scilly. All are open at any
time without charge, though a landing fee is charged at Tresco.

St. Mary's, Bants Carn Burial Chamber and Ancient Village

A Bronze Age burial mound with entrance passage and chamber. Nearby
are the remains of round and oval stone huts forming a village which was
occupied in the middle of the Roman period.

Situation: 1 mile north of Hugh Town.

St. Mary's, Harry's Walls

A sixteenth-century fort built to command the harbour of St. Mary's Pool.
Situation: ¼ mile north-east of Hugh Town.

St. Mary's, Innisidgen Burial Chamber

A small Bronze Age burial mound with well-built chamber.
Situation: 1¾ miles north-east of Hugh Town.

St. Mary's, Lower Innisidgen Burial Chamber

A Bronze Age passage grave. Not yet completely excavated.
Situation: 1¾ miles north-east of Hugh Town.

St. Mary's, Porth Hellick Down Burial Chamber

Probably the best preserved Bronze Age burial mound on the Islands, with entrance passage and chamber.
Situation: 1½ miles east of Hugh Town.

Tresco, Cromwell's Castle

A round tower built about the middle of the seventeenth century to house guns commanding the haven of New Grimsby. Alterations were made to it after the Civil War and again in the eighteenth century.
Situation: About 200 yards south-west of King Charles's Castle.

Tresco, King Charles's Castle

A castle built probably during the reign of Edward VI for coast defence. Additional fortifications were built during the Civil War.
Situation: ¾ mile north-west of New Grimsby.

Tresco, Old Blockhouse

Built towards the end of the sixteenth century as a battery for artillery.
Situation: On Block House Point, at the south end of Old Grimsby Harbour.

DEVON

**Blackbury Castle, Southleigh*

An oval-shaped camp defended by a single bank and ditch with a complicated entrance on its southern side; probably of the Iron Age.

Situation: 1½ miles south-west of Southleigh.

Admission: At any time.

**Dartmouth, Bayard's Cove Castle*

A sixteenth-century fortlet, covering the entrance to the inner haven.

Situation: In Dartmouth, at the south end of Bayard's Cove.

Admission: At any time.

†*Dartmouth Castle* (Plate 14)

A small fifteenth-century fort, largely added to in the last quarter of the sixteenth century. It still had a Governor and was maintained in a fair state of repair until the middle of the last century.

Situation: 1 mile south-east of Dartmouth.

Hours of Admission: Standard, but Sundays from 9.30 a.m., May to September.

**†*Lydford Castle*

A late twelfth-century keep with a rectangular bailey on its western side within the area of a Saxon burh. The castle was the seat of the Stannary Court until the court was moved to Princetown in the beginning of the last century.

Situation: In Lydford.

Admission: At any time.

†*Okehampton Castle*

Founded in the eleventh century, but very largely reconstructed in the early fourteenth, and dismantled on the death of the Marquis of Exeter in 1539. It takes advantage of a naturally fortified ridge and consists of a series of courts lined by buildings leading to a rectangular keep at the highest point.

Situation: 1 mile south-west of Okehampton.

Admission: Standard, but Sundays from 9.30 a.m., May to September.

Mount Batton Castle, Plymstock

A tower 30 ft. high with original windows and vaulted roof. Built in 1665 and named after Captain Batton, Governor of Plymouth during the Civil War.

Situation: On an island in Plymouth Harbour.

Admission: Access one day a month, with prior application to Officer Commanding, RAF, Plymouth, PL9 9SH.

†*Paignton, Kirkham House*

A fourteenth-century stone house.

Situation: In Kirkham Street.

Hours of Admission: Standard, April to September.

Plymouth, Citadel

The Citadel is a large fortification erected after the Restoration. The elaborate entrance gateway is dated 1670. Inside is a statue of George II in classical armour.

Situation: To the east of Hoe Park.

Admission: On application to the military authorities.

†*Totnes Castle

A large Norman motte-and-bailey castle, founded by Judhael in the time of the Conqueror. It was provided with a stone shell-keep and curtain wall in the early thirteenth century, and these were reconstructed on the original pattern in the early fourteenth century. The keep is still remarkably complete.

Situation: On top of the hill, on the slopes of which the borough stands.

Hours of Admission: Standard.

DORSET

**Abbotsbury, Abbey Buildings*

The eastern gable of one of the conventional buildings of Abbotsbury Abbey.

Situation: In Abbotsbury, just south of the churchyard.

Admission: At any time.

Abbotsbury, St. Catherine's Chapel

A small fifteenth-century chapel with a fine decorated stone vault. Extensive views can be obtained in every direction from the turret which was used as a beacon tower.

Situation: ½ mile south of Abbotsbury, on the hill-top.

Hours of Admission: Not at present open to the public.

Fiddleford Mill House

A fourteenth-century house, altered in the early sixteenth century, comprising a hall and a solar block, both with highly elaborate roofs.

Situation: 1 mile east of Sturminster Newton.

Admission: Not yet open to the public.

**Jordan Hill Roman Temple, Preston*

Foundations of a small rectangular Romano-Celtic temple.

Situation: 2 miles north-east of Weymouth.

Admission: At any time.

**Kingston Russell Stone Circle*

A prehistoric circle of eighteen stones.

Situation: 2 miles north of Abbotsbury.

Admission: At any time.

Knowlton Church and Earthworks

A "Henge" monument, consisting of a circular ditch with a bank on the outside, probably originally containing a timber circle (compare Woodhenge), but now containing a ruined church of Norman origin.

Situation: 3 miles south-west of Cranborne.

Admission: At any time.

**†*Maiden Castle, Dorchester* (Plate 4)

The finest known example of a prehistoric fortress in this country, with enormous earthworks and complicated entrances. It dates from the Iron Age and superseded a neolithic camp. The remains of a fourth-century Roman temple have been discovered within the fortifications.

Situation: 2½ miles south-west of Dorchester.

Admission: At any time.

Plate 17. Muchelney Abbey

Plate 18. Netley Abbey

Plate 19. Old Wardour Castle

Plate 20. Greenwich, Queen's House

*Portland Castle

Erected by Henry VIII for coast defence and added to in the seventeenth century.

Situation: Overlooking Portland Harbour.

Hours of Admission: Standard, April to September.

†Sherborne Old Castle

Built by Roger, Bishop of Salisbury between 1107 and 1135. The keep and curtain wall with its towers and gates belong to this period. The castle came in 1592 into the hands of Sir Walter Raleigh who was responsible for some minor alterations.

Situation: ½ mile east of Sherborne.

Admission: Standard.

**The Nine Stones, Winterborne Abbas

Remains of a prehistoric stone circle consisting of nine standing stones.

Situation: South of the road about ½ mile west of Winterborne Abbas.

Admission: At any time.

Winterborne Poor Lot Barrows

A fine group of Bowl, Bell and Disc barrows of the Bronze Age.

Situation: 2 miles west of Winterborne Abbas.

Admission: At any time.

HAMPSHIRE

†Bishop's Waltham Palace

Extensive ruins of a palace of the Bishops of Winchester, founded by Bishop Henry of Blois in the mid-twelfth century. The surviving buildings, grouped about a quadrangular courtyard and enclosed by a moat, include a corner tower and hall range of the end of the twelfth century, with subsequent alterations culminating in the reconstruction by Bishop Langton in the 1490s.

Situation: In Bishop's Waltham.

Hours of Admission: Standard but closed Mondays (unless a Bank Holiday).

Calshot Castle

Erected by Henry VIII for coast defence and subsequently modified.

Situation: On a pebble spit in the south-west corner of Southampton Water, 2 miles south-west of Fawley.

Admission: Not yet open to the public.

**†*Christchurch Castle, Keep and Norman House*

A rectangular tower on a Norman motte, also the first-floor hall of the castle, built *c.* 1160, and retaining some original windows and a Norman chimney.

Situation: In Christchurch.

Admission: Standard.

†*Hurst Castle*

Erected by Henry VIII for coast defence and added to in the eighteenth and nineteenth centuries.

Situation: 2½ miles south-east of Milford Church on a pebble spit; usually approached by sea from Key Haven.

Hours of Admission: Standard.

†*Netley Abbey* (Plate 18)

Extensive and beautiful remains of a Cistercian abbey founded in 1239. The walls of the greater part of the church and of the claustral buildings still stand as well as a remarkable medieval (abbot's?) house, and there is much fine thirteenth-century architectural detail.

Situation: in Netley.

Hours of Admission: Standard.

†*Portchester Castle* (Plate 6)

A large Roman fortress of the late third century, of which practically the whole of the walls and bastions are standing. There is a medieval castle in the north-west angle with a fine and practically perfect Norman keep. The Norman church of an Augustinian priory also stands within the Roman walls.

Situation: On the south side of Portchester.

Hours of Admission: Standard, but Sundays from 9.30 a.m., May to September.

**Portsmouth, Garrison Church*

This church was originally a hospital, founded by Bishop des Roches in 1214. The fine thirteenth-century chancel was the hospital chapel. The nave, which is much rebuilt, was badly damaged by enemy action in the war.

Situation: On Grand Parade to the south of High Street.

Admission: To the chancel, which is in use as the garrison church.

**Portsmouth (a) King James's Gate*
(b) Landport Gate

Two gates of the defences of Portsmouth which were begun in 1665 by Charles II. The former was completed in 1687, the latter in 1698.

Situation: (a) Re-erected at the entrance to the officers' recreation ground.

(b) In its original position, now forming the entrance to the men's recreation ground.

Admission: Can be seen from the public streets.

Silchester Roman Town Walls

The very complete circuit of walls, built, probably in the Severan period, round the Romano–British tribal capital of Calleva Atrebatum.

Situation: Around and to the west of Silchester, six miles north of Basingstoke.

Admission: Not yet open to the public.

†*Titchfield Abbey* (Plate 16)

Founded as a house of Premonstratensian Canons in 1232, dissolved in 1537 and converted into a mansion by Thomas Wriothesley, Earl of Southampton. The south range and gatehouse of the mansion which were incorporated in the nave of the monastic church are still practically complete. There are also remains of the chapter house and other monastic buildings.

Situation: ½ mile north of Titchfield.

Hours of Admission: Standard.

Wolvesey Castle, Winchester

Ruins of an extensive palace of the Bishops of Winchester, built round a quadrangular courtyard; much of the original work of Bishop Henry of Blois in the mid-twelfth century still stands including a square keep and part of a great hall, very advanced in design.

Situation: At the south-east corner of Winchester.

Admission: Not yet open to the public.

ISLE OF WIGHT

†*Appuldurcombe*

The shell of a fine house begun by Sir Robert Worsley in 1710, close to the site of a cell of the Norman abbey of Montebourg. It was completed by Sir Richard Worsley who installed in it the celebrated Museum Worsleianum of paintings and classical antiquities, now dispersed. The house became unoccupied in 1909.

Situation: ½ mile west of Wroxall.

Hours of Admission: Standard.

†**Carisbrooke Castle* (Plate 11)

An extensive and important medieval castle of motte-and-bailey plan begun in the late eleventh century, subsequently provided with a Norman curtain wall and "shell"-keep, and altered and added to later. Underlying the castle are the remains of a late Roman fort. Charles I was imprisoned here 1647–8. The Governor's Lodge houses the Isle of Wight County Museum.

Situation: 1¼ miles south-west of Newport.

Hours of Admission: Standard, but Sundays, May to September, 2 to 5.30 p.m.

***Chale, St. Catherine's Chapel*

The west tower, used as a beacon, of a chapel of St. Catherine founded early in the fourteenth century as a result of the wreck of the wine-ship *Ste. Marie* of Bayonne.

Situation: ¾ mile north-west of Niton.

Admission: At any time.

†*Osborne House

Built as a private residence by Queen Victoria in 1845–6, with additions made during the second half of the nineteenth century. The Queen died here in 1901, having spent much of her married life and widowhood at the house.

The house is used as a Convalescent Home for Officers and is maintained by the Ministry. The grounds, Queen Victoria's State Apartments, and the Swiss Cottage Museum are open to the public.

Situation: 1 mile south-east of Cowes.

Hours of Admission: Easter Monday to beginning of October: Mondays to Fridays 11 a.m. to 5.30 p.m.

†*Yarmouth Castle

The latest of Henry VIII's chain of coastal castles, totally different from others and including the earliest pointed bastion in England.

Situation: In Yarmouth.

Hours of Admission: Standard.

KENT

†*Canterbury, St. Augustine's Abbey

Founded by St. Augustine on land given by King Ethelbert in 598. The foundations of the seventh-century church of Saints Peter and Paul, which was the burial place of the early Archbishops and Kings of Kent, and the remains of an eleventh-century round church underlie the extensive ruins of the medieval Benedictine abbey.

Situation: In Canterbury.

Hours of Admission: Standard, but Sundays from 9.30 a.m., May to September.

*Canterbury, St. Pancras's Church

Founded by St. Augustine at the end of the sixth century. The nave and porticus are built of re-used Roman bricks. The chancel was reconstructed in the fourteenth century.

Situation: In Canterbury, east of St. Augustine's Abbey.

Hours of Admission: Standard, but Sundays from 9.30 a.m., May to September.

Admission Fee: Included in the admission to St. Augustine's Abbey.

†*Deal Castle

The largest and most complete of the series of castles built by Henry VIII for coast defence.

Situation: In Deal.

Hours of Admission: Standard, but Sundays from 9.30 a.m., May to September.

†*_Dover Castle_ (Plates 9 and 10)

One of the largest and most important English castles. The keep, latest and finest of the great Norman square towers, is surpassed in size only by those of London and Colchester. The great thickness of the walls permitted the construction of twenty-seven mural chambers within them, a number without parallel in any other English keep. In the forebuilding are two ornate chapels of the late twelfth century. The double curtain walls include a splendid series of gates and towers. A Roman lighthouse and Saxon church stand within the castle.

Situation: On the east side of Dover.

Hours of Admission: Keep, standard, but Sundays from 9.30 a.m., May to September; grounds and underground passages, standard on week-days, Sundays 10 a.m. to sunset.

Dover, Western Heights Fortifications

These fortifications, which were begun _c._ 1779 but not completed until 1860, were intended to be the largest and strongest in the country, sufficient to hold a great body of troops in case of invasion of the Romney Marsh area.

Situation: On the west side of Dover.

Admission: Not yet open to the public.

**_Dover, Knights Templars' Church_

The foundations of a small circular twelfth-century church.

Situation: On the Western Heights above Dover.

Admission: On application to the military authorities.

Dymchurch, Martello Tower

One of a series of circular towers erected for coastal defence in 1805–10, with mountings for a heavy gun on the roof.

Situation: In Dymchurch.

Admission: Standard.

**_Ebbsfleet, St. Augustine's Cross_

A modern cross marking the traditional site of the landing of St. Augustine in 597.

Situation: 2 miles east of Minster.

Admission: At any time.

†*Eynsford Castle*

A twelfth-century castle with the greater part of a high curtain wall and a stone hall.

Situation: In Eynsford.

Hours of Admission: Standard.

Horne's Place Chapel, Appledore

A fourteenth-century domestic chapel with undercroft, once attached to the manor house.

Situation: 1 mile north of Appledore.

Admission: Not yet open to the public.

**(*a*) *Kit's Coty House, Aylesford*

The chamber of a prehistoric long barrow or burial place. The barrow originally consisted of a long earthen mound covering the chamber which contained the human remains.

**(*b*) *Little Kit's Coty House, Aylesford*

A ruined burial chamber of a prehistoric barrow.

Situation: (*a*) On the west side of the Maidstone–Rochester road, 3½ miles north of Maidstone.

(*b*) ½ mile south of (*a*) on the east side of the Aylesford road.

Admission: At any time.

†*Lullingstone Roman Villa*

A large country house, occupied through much of the Roman period and revealing four distinct phases of building, to the last two of which belong the splendid mosaics in the reception rooms and the unique remains of a Christian chapel.

Situation: Half a mile north-west of Eynsford station.

Hours of Admission: Standard, but Sundays from 9.30 a.m., May to September.

†*Old Soar Manor, Plaxtol*

A fine example of a late thirteenth-century house, with solar over vaulted undercroft, and chapel. The hall has been replaced by an eighteenth-century farm-house. National Trust property, placed in guardianship of the Ministry.

Situation: About 6 miles north-north-east of Tonbridge and 1 mile east of Plaxtol village.

Hours of Admission: Standard, April to September.

†Ospringe, Maison Dieu

An early sixteenth-century timber-framed building incorporating an ancillary building of a hospital founded by Henry III. It contains a small museum.

Situation: In Ospringe village, ½ mile west of Faversham.

Hours of Admission: Standard.

†*Reculver Towers and Roman Fort

The remains of a Saxon church founded in the seventh century standing within the walls of a Roman fortress. The early church was altered and enlarged during the Middle Ages and the towers are of late twelfth-century date.

Situation: At Reculver, 3 miles east of Herne Bay.

Hours of Admission: To church: Standard, but Sundays from 9.30 a.m., May to September. Fort walls: At any time.

**Richborough Amphitheatre

An amphitheatre serving the Roman fort at Richborough, and measuring 200 ft. by 166 ft. Not yet excavated.

Situation: ¼ mile south-west of Richborough Castle.

Admission: At any time.

†*Richborough Castle (Plate 5)

The Roman invading army landed here in A.D. 43 and a stretch of earthworks then thrown up can be seen. The site became a military supply depot during the advance. Towards the end of the first century a large monument was erected, probably to commemorate the conquest of Britain. In the late third century a fort was built here and its massive walls still stand to a height of 25 feet. In Saxon times a chapel to St. Augustine, who is reputed to have landed here, was built within the walls.

Situation: 1½ miles north of Sandwich.

Hours of Admission: Standard, but Sundays from 9.30 a.m., May to September.

†Rochester, Temple Manor, Strood

The thirteenth-century great chamber, on a vaulted undercroft, of a manor house of the Knights Templars. Extensive additions have mostly been demolished.

Situation: On the west bank of the Medway, ½ mile south-west of Rochester Bridge.

Hours of Admission: Standard.

†Rochester Castle

A large single enclosure begun by Bishop Gundulf in the late eleventh century and partly founded on the Roman city wall, enclosing a splendid square keep of *c.* 1130. The north-west angles of both were rebuilt after a siege in 1215.

Situation: On the east bank of the Medway just south of Rochester Bridge.

Hours of Admission: Standard.

†Upnor Castle

A blockhouse for the defence of the Medway estuary, built 1560–63 and altered later, presenting a large pointed bastion to the river and a gate-tower to the land.

Situation: 1¾ miles north-east of Strood.

Hours of Admission: Standard.

†*Walmer Castle

One of the series of castles for coast defence built by Henry VIII. The castle is the residence of the Lord Warden of the Cinque Ports.
The rooms occupied by the Duke of Wellington, who spent his last days here, still contain his furniture and have been preserved unaltered.

Situation: South of Walmer.

Hours of Admission: Standard, but Sundays from 9.30 a.m., May to September when the Lord Warden is not in residence. The gardens are closed during the winter months.

**West Malling, St. Leonard's Tower

A fine early Norman tower built by Gundulf, Bishop of Rochester.

Situation: ¼ mile south-west of West Malling.

Admission: At any time, on application to the caretaker.

LONDON (South of Thames)

†Eltham Palace

A royal manor from the thirteenth century, most of the buildings were rebuilt from the time of Edward IV onwards. The splendid late fifteenth-century great hall survives with its hammer-beam roof, as does the bridge

F

over the moat, while the foundations of buildings along the curtain wall
have been excavated.

Situation: South-west of Eltham High Street.

Admission: Thursday and Sunday only. May to October, 11 a.m. to 7 p.m.;
November to April, 11 a.m. to 4 p.m.

** *Greenwich Royal Naval College

The Royal Naval College occupied the buildings of the Hospital founded in
1694 for disabled seamen of the Royal Navy. The Painted Hall, designed by
Wren and completed by Vanbrugh as a dining-hall, was decorated by
Thornhill between 1708 and 1727 with allegorical paintings. The chapel,
which was burnt in 1797, was restored by the architect James Stuart.
*Postcards on sale at the Queen's House, Greenwich.

Situation: On Thames-side at Greenwich.

Hours of Admission: Weekdays, 2.30 p.m. to 5 p.m. (closed on Thursdays);
Sundays, May to the end of September, 2.30 p.m. to 5 p.m.

Greenwich Royal Observatory

Flamsteed House was built under a Royal Warrant of 1675 establishing a
Royal Observatory for "the finding out the longitude of places for perfecting
navigation and astronomy". Its site was formerly occupied by Greenwich
Castle, a tower built by Humphrey, Duke of Gloucester, and repaired or
rebuilt by Henry VIII in 1526. Sir Christopher Wren was in charge of the
work and the Reverend John Flamsteed, after whom the house is now called,
was the first Astronomer Royal. A stone mark, north of the building, marks
the position of the zero meridian of longitude.

Situation: In Greenwich Park.

Admission: Not yet open to the public.

** *Queen's House, Greenwich (Plate 20)

This house was designed by Inigo Jones and completed in 1635 and is an
outstanding example of his work. It was enlarged in 1662. Additions made
in the early nineteenth century, when the house was granted to the Greenwich
Hospital School, have been removed; much of the original decoration has
been exposed. It now contains part of the collection of the National Maritime
Museum.

Situation: On the north side of Greenwich Park.

Hours of Admission: Weekdays, 10 a.m. to 6 p.m.; Sundays, 2.30 p.m. to
6 p.m. In winter the house is closed at dusk.

SOMERSET

**Charlcombe, Sir Bevil Granville's Monument*

An early eighteenth-century monument to Sir Bevil Granville, slain at the battle of Lansdown, 1643.

Situation: On Lansdown Hill, near road to Wick, 4 miles north-west of Bath.

Admission: At any time.

†*Cleeve Abbey*

A Cistercian abbey founded by William de Roumara, Earl of Lincoln, towards the end of the twelfth century. Only the foundations of the church remain, but the greater part of the claustral buildings survives almost intact and includes the frater with a fine timber roof. The gatehouse was built by the last abbot.

Situation: At the south end of Washford village.

Hours of Admission: Standard.

**Dunster, Butter Cross*

A stone cross, said to have been moved from Dunster High Street. Also known as Rockhead Cross.

Situation: Beside the road to Alcombe, 400 yards north-west of Dunster parish church.

Admission: At any time.

**Dunster, Gallox Bridge*

A stone packhorse bridge with two ribbed arches, in picturesque surroundings.

Situation: At the southern end of Dunster.

Admission: At any time.

**Dunster, Yarn Market*

An octagonal market hall, built by the Luttrells of Dunster Castle in 1609 and repaired in 1647. It was used for the sale of cloth woven locally.

Situation: In the High Street.

Admission: At any time.

†*Farleigh Castle

Dates from the late fourteenth century and consists of two courts defended by a moat, walls and towers. In the outer court is the chapel containing a fine tomb of Sir Thomas Hungerford, the builder of the castle.

Situation: In Farleigh Hungerford, 3½ miles west of Trowbridge (Wilts.).
Hours of Admission: Standard.

†*Glastonbury Tribunal

The fifteenth-century courthouse of Glastonbury Abbey, re-fronted by Abbot Bere between 1493 and 1524.

Situation: In High Street, Glastonbury.
Hours of Admission: Standard.

**Meare, Abbot's Fish House

A fourteenth-century building used in connection with the fishery of Glastonbury Abbey.

Situation: At the eastern end of Meare village.
Admission: At any time.

†*Muchelney Abbey (Plate 17)

Part of the claustral buildings of this medieval Benedictine abbey still stand in a very complete state. They consist of the south walk of the cloister, part of the frater, the kitchen and the abbot's lodging. There is some fine detail of the fifteenth and early sixteenth centuries. Excavations have revealed the plan of the abbey church and of its immediate predecessor.

Situation: In Muchelney, 2 miles south of Langport.
Hours of Admission: Standard.

†*Nunney Castle (Plate 13)

A small but very complete late fourteenth-century castle of French patterns consisting of a compact tower with large round towers at the angles, standing in a moat. It fell to the Parliamentarians in 1645 on the second day of the siege.

Situation: In Nunnery, about 3½ miles south-west of Frome.
Hours of Admission: Standard.

†*Stanton Drew Circles and Cove*

Three prehistoric stone circles, the remains of two avenues of standing stones and a prehistoric burial chamber. One of the finest monuments of this description in the country, and probably of the same date as Avebury.

Situation: Circles, to the east of the village of Stanton Drew. Cove, in the garden of the Druid's Arms.

Hours of Admission: At any time on weekdays.

†*Stoney Littleton Long Barrow*

A prehistoric burial place consisting of a long earthen mound containing a long passage with recesses on both sides where the human remains were deposited. The walls of the passage and recesses are of dry-built masonry roofed with large slabs of stone. A tablet on the monument records its restoration in 1858.

Situation: 1 mile south of Wellow.

Admission: On application at Stoney Littleton Farm.

SURREY

†**Farnham Castle*

A castle of the Bishops of Winchester, of motte-and-bailey plan. The large "shell"-keep is open to the public; it encloses a mound in which are the massive substructures of an earlier Norman square tower. The bailey buildings are still occupied. The castle was a scene of fighting in the Civil War.

Situation: In Farnham.

Hours of Admission: Standard.

†*Ham House, Petersham*

Begun *c.* 1610, this famous early seventeenth-century house was enlarged after the Restoration when it was the residence of the Duke of Lauderdale. Its almost unrivalled contemporary furnishings are in the care of the Victoria and Albert Museum. The house is National Trust property and is maintained by the Ministry.

Situation: In Petersham, 1½ miles south of Richmond.

Hours of Admission: Summer, 2 p.m. to 6 p.m.; winter, noon to 4 p.m. Closed on Mondays other than Bank Holidays.

†*Kew Palace

An early seventeenth-century house built for a London merchant. Bought by George III in 1781, it was the residence of royalty until the death of Queen Charlotte in 1818.

Situation: Inside the Royal Botanic Gardens, Kew.

Hours of Admission: April to September, weekdays, 11 a.m. to 6 p.m.; Sundays, 1 p.m. to 6 p.m.

Waverley Abbey

The earliest Cistercian house in England, founded by Bishop Gifford in 1128. The upstanding remains are of thirteenth-century date.

Situation: Beside the Wey, 2 miles east of Farnham.

Admission: Not yet open to the public.

SUSSEX

Bayham Abbey, Frant

Impressive ruins of a house of Premonstratensian Canons, founded about 1208 and dissolved under Wolsey in 1525. The eastern arm of the church is unusually elaborate.

Situation: 1¾ miles west of Lamberhurst.

Admission: Not yet open to the public.

Hurstmonceux Castle

A quadrilateral moated castle of brick dating from *c.* 1440; once ruinous and twice restored, the internal buildings are recent and not accessible to the public, but the very impressive exterior is little altered.

Situation: One mile south of Hurstmonceux.

Admission: To view exterior only, at convenience of the Royal Observatory.

†*Pevensey Castle (Plate 7)

Extensive remains of a large late Roman fortress of exceptional plan. In the late eleventh century a castle was built in the eastern end of the Roman fortress, and there are considerable remains of an unusual keep and fine thirteenth-century curtain walls, towers and gatehouse.

Situation: In Pevensey.

Hours of Admission: Standard.

WILTSHIRE

†*Avebury* (Plate 1)

A complex and gigantic megalithic monument of the beginning of the Bronze Age, originally consisting of two or perhaps three stone circles. Later in the same period, an outer stone circle and bank and ditch were constructed. Many stones were destroyed or cast down in the seventeenth and eighteenth centuries; some have been re-erected and the sites of others marked with concrete blocks. The West Kennet Avenue of standing stones (some re-erected) runs southwards to the Sanctuary, Overton Hill (see below). National Trust property in the guardianship of the Ministry.

Situation: 7 miles west of Marlborough.

Hours of Admission: To the Museum, standard, but Sundays from 9.30 a.m., May to September. To the site, at any time without charge.

**†*Bradford-on-Avon Tithe Barn*

A fine fourteenth-century barn which belonged to Shaftesbury Abbey.

Situation: At Barton Farm, ¼ mile south of Bradford-on-Avon.

Admission: At any time.

**Bratton Camp and White Horse, Westbury*

A large prehistoric camp probably of the Iron Age with a long barrow of earlier date within the fortifications. The White Horse cut in the turf below the camp is in its present form of eighteenth-century date.

Situation: 1 mile south-west of Bratton and 2 miles east of Westbury.

Admission: At any time.

**Ludgershall Castle and Cross*

A Norman castle of which extensive earthworks and a complex but very ruinous series of buildings exists. The village cross, in the main street, is also in the Ministry's charge.

Situation: On the north side of Ludgershall.

Admission: At any time.

**Netheravon Dovecote*

An eighteenth-century brick dovecote retaining most of its chalk nesting-boxes.

Situation: In Netheravon, 4½ miles north of Amesbury.

Admission: At any time, on application at Netheravon House.

†*Old Sarum (Plate 8)

Probably originally an Iron Age hill-fort, then a Saxon burh, and Norman town. The enormous and extensive earthworks are of late eleventh-century date. Excavation has revealed extensive remains of the castle and cathedral. The latter was moved to Salisbury between 1220 and 1230. A small museum containing architectural fragments is on the site.

Situation: 2 miles north of Salisbury.

Hours of Admission: Standard, but Sundays from 9.30 a.m. May to September.

*Old Wardour Castle (Plate 19)

A hexagonal castle surrounding a central courtyard, built by John, Lord Lovel, in 1392, with alterations in the Renaissance style added after 1570. The west side was blown up during the siege in the Civil War.

Situation: In Wardour Park, 2 miles south-west of Tisbury.

Hours of Admission: Standard.

**Silbury Hill, Avebury

An artificial prehistoric mound, the largest existing example of this type in Europe. Believed to be sepulchral, and probably dating from Early Bronze Age.

Situation: Beside the Bath road, 1 mile west of the village of West Kennet.

Admission: At any time.

†*Stonehenge (Plate 3)

A prehistoric monument of world-wide fame, consisting of a series of stone circles, one within another, all being surrounded by a ditch and bank and approached by an "avenue" on the east side. The disposition of the stone circles was changed several times within the early Bronze Age.

Situation: 2 miles west of Amesbury.

Hours of Admission: Standard, but Sundays from 9.30 a.m., March to September.

**The Sanctuary, Overton Hill

The West Kennet Avenue of standing stones connected this monument with Avebury. The sanctuary consisted of two concentric circles of stones and six of timber uprights, the sites of which are marked by low concrete pillars. It was erected probably in the Early Bronze Age.

Situation: Beside the Bath road, ½ mile east of the village of West Kennet.

Admission: At any time.

****†*West Kennet Long Barrow***

A prehistoric burial place near Avebury consisting of a long earthen mound containing a passage with side chambers in which the human remains were placed. The entrance was afterwards blocked by a large stone.

Situation: ¾ mile south-west of the village of West Kennet.

Admission: At any time.

****†*Windmill Hill***

A neolithic habitation site including a "causewayed camp", excavated in the 1920s. The finds then made are in Avebury Museum. National Trust property in the guardianship of the Ministry.

Situation: 1½ miles north-west of Avebury.

Admission: At any time.

*****Woodhenge, Durrington**

This monument consisted of six concentric rings of timber posts, now marked by concrete stumps, surrounded by a ditch with a bank on the outside. It was entered by a causeway on the north-west. The rings are oval, the long axis pointing to the rising sun on Midsummer Day.

Situation: Beside the Pewsey road, 2 miles north of Amesbury.

Admission: At any time.

BIBLIOGRAPHY

General

THE COUNTY HISTORY SERIES (Darwen Finlayson):

    Hampshire. *Carpenter-Turner, B.* 1963.

    Kent. *Jessup, F. W.* 1958.

    Sussex. *Armstrong, J. R.* 1961.

PEVSNER, N., THE BUILDINGS OF ENGLAND:

    Berkshire. 1966.

    Cornwall. 1951.

    Devon, 1952.

    Hampshire, 1967.

    Kent, 1969

    Somerset. 1958.

    Surrey. 1952.

    Sussex. 1965.

    Wiltshire. 1963.

ROYAL COMMISSION ON HISTORICAL MONUMENTS:

    Dorset, vol. 1 (West). 1952.

SORREL, A. Living History. 1965.

SURREY COUNTY COUNCIL:

    Antiquities of Surrey. 5th ed., 1965.

Prehistoric Period

ASHBEE, P. The Bronze Age Round Barrow in Britain. 1960.

ATKINSON, R. J. C. Stonehenge. 1956.

CLARK, J. D. G. Prehistoric England, Paperback ed. 1962.

DANIEL, G. E. The Prehistoric Chamber-tombs of England and Wales. 1950

FOWLER, P. Wessex, 1967.

FOX, C. The Personality of Britain. 1947.

FOX, A. South West England. 1964.

GRINSELL, L. V. The Ancient Burial Mounds of England. 2nd ed., 1953.

           The Archæology of Wessex. 1958.

ORDNANCE SURVEY. Map of Southern Britain in the Iron Age. 1962.

ROE, D. Prehistory, 1969.

THOMAS, N. Guide to Prehistoric England. 1960.

WHEELER, R. E. M. Maiden Castle, Dorset. 1943.

Roman Period

BOON, G. C. Roman Silchester. 1957.

BUSHE-FOX, J. P. AND OTHERS. Excavations . . . at Richborough. 1926 ff. esp. vol. v (1968).

FRERE, S.S. Britannia.

MARGARY, I. D. Roman Roads in Britain, vol. 1 (South). 1955.

MOTHERSOLE, J. The Saxon Shore, 1924.

ORDNANCE SURVEY. Map of Roman Britain. 3rd ed., 1956.

RICHMOND, I. A. Roman Britain (Pelican History). 1955.

RIVET, A. L. F. Town and Country in Roman Britain. 1958.
    The Roman Villa in Britain, 1969.

Anglo-Saxon Period

CLAPHAM, A. W. English Romanesque Architecture before the Conquest. 1930.

HODKIN, R. H. History of the Anglo-Saxons. 3rd ed., 1952.

MYRES, J. N. L. Anglo-Saxon Pottery and the settlement of England, 1969.

ORDNANCE SURVEY. Map of Dark-Age Britain. 2nd ed., 1966.

TAYLOR, H. M. and J. Anglo-Saxon Architecture. 1965.

WILSON, D. The Anglo-Saxons. 1960.

Medieval Period, General

THE HISTORY OF THE KING'S WORKS (H.M.S.O.): Part 1, the Middle Ages. 1963.

BERESFORD, M. W. and ST. JOSEPH, J. K. Medieval England, an Aerial Survey. 1958.

SALZMAN, L. F. Building in England to 1540. 1952.

WOOD, M. E. The English Medieval House. 1965.

Monastic Buildings

CLAPHAM, A. W. English Romanesque Architecture after the Conquest. 1934.

DICKINSON, J. C. Monastic Life in Medieval England. 1961.

GILYARD-BEER, R. Abbeys. 1958.

JAMES, M. R. Abbeys. 1926.

KNOWLES, D., and HADCOCK, R. N. Medieval Religious Houses. 1953.

KNOWLES, D. and ST. JOSEPH, J. K. Monastic Sites from the Air. 1952.
ORDNANCE SURVEY. Map of Monastic Britain (South). 2nd ed., 1954.
THOMPSON, A. H. English Monasteries. 1923.

Fortifications

ARMITAGE, E. S. Early Norman Castles. 1912.
BROWN, R. A. English Medieval Castles. 1954.
O'NEIL, B. H. ST. J. Castles. 1953.
        Castles and Cannon. 1960.
THOMPSON, A. H. Military Architecture in England during the Middle Ages.
    1912.

INDEX

Printed in England for Her Majesty's Stationery Office
by The Campfield Press, St. Albans

Dd. 501325 K54 11/70